Evolution

A Revolutionary Journey

DARRICK JOHNSON

Copyright © 2020 Darrick Johnson

All rights reserved.

ISBN: 978-1-7348113-3-9

Contents

TESTIMONIALS

DEDICATION

INTRODUCTION 1

CHAPTER 1: THE HEALING THERAPY IN WRITING 11

CHAPTER 2: MENTAL STABILITY 23

CHAPTER 3: WE ALL WEAR THE MASK; IT'S NEITHER GOOD NOR BAD! 33

CHAPTER 4: STRONG PEOPLE DON'T SHOW STRENGTH IN FRONT OF US RATHER, IT'S SHOWN BY THOSE WHO WIN BATTLES MOST KNOW NOTHING ABOUT. 37

CHAPTER 5: PEACE BEGINS WITH ME 45

CHAPTER 6: INFORMATION IS POWER 49

CHAPTER 7: PEACE AND CLOSURE 53

CHAPTER 8: THE POWER OF FORGIVENESS 63

CHAPTER 9: SAYING GOODBYE TO YESTERDAY IS HARD 73

CHAPTER 10: REAPING BENEFITS FROM A NOT SO PLEASANT PAST 79

CHAPTER 11: POST-TRAUMATIC SYNDROME AND BLACK HEALTH 87

CHAPTER 12: BREAKING THE CHAINS OF CULTURAL CONFORMITY BASED ON HIS-STORY 93

CHAPTER 13: RADICAL TRANSFORMATION	97
CHAPTER 14: AMERICA HAS YET TO REACH GREATNESS	103
EPILOGUE: CHANGE, REFORM AND ACCOUNTABILITY - BLACK LIVES MATTER	111
POETRY	115

Testimonials

We met serving in the US Marine Corps; I called him Drago, after the Russian boxer in the Rocky movie, partly because he boxed and wore a flattop, but mostly because his fuse remained lit. Drago was quick-tempered, angry, and aggressive, and many chose to keep a safe distance. We became brothers, and I got to know and see the man beneath the anger. He was funny, caring, protective, and the most conscientious black man I knew. He was aware of every action and the impact it had on others and society even amid doing wrong. Darrick is the perfect illustration of personal reflection and accountability. The man I see today, the father, grandfather, and social activist, is, in many ways, the same man I knew as Drago. He is now more comfortable letting the world see it!

Respectfully,

Clifford R. Brown
Executive Officer
Public Assistance Division
Recovery Directorate

My sister Muhsina and I facilitate a spiritually based group known as First Sunday. When Darrick got up to speak at our gathering, we reminded ourselves how often we had welcomed men to join us, to add that "male energy" to the group. Well boy, did we get more "energy" than we expected! Darrick shared the male side of an emotionally devastating breakup with such candor and honesty that we were all healed in the process. He kept coming back, and he brought his young daughters with him, where they got the chance to witness him channel his anger. His children often mentioned his "too serious" persona, which molded him into becoming the talented writer and performer that he is today.

Janice Ellis
Life coach, facilitator of First Sunday

An inspirational brother, and talented too. Darrick Johnson has so much knowledge, so much for you! His wisdom is growing, his passion is strong and you will benefit greatly. When you listen, you will never go wrong… A litany of lessons that he's learned firsthand. With knowledge as power, the better we all stand! A fierce yet humble warrior, his word is his bond. Trust him, you have got this… the strength to go on. A brilliant, dynamic and talented brother who always inspires, while continuing our legacy of greatness; first in our ancient history and then in our personal growth, enlightenment and enrichment. I've enjoyed being a part of his journey!

Nana Malaya
Artistic Director of Nubian (Theater Dance & Music Company)
"The Dancing Diplomat"

Evolution is the process of a living organism's development from its original form over time. For the last several years, I've had the privilege of watching a fragment of Darrick Johnson's evolution as a man, husband, father, brother, and friend. To see a man openly share his vulnerabilities, faults and failures for the greater good of others is unusual, because men tend to hold their frailties close to the vest. However, Darrick willingly shared his wounds with our men's group while simultaneously using his God-given wisdom to help prevent men from making similar missteps. One will enjoy reading a more in-depth composition of Darrick Johnson's evolution.

Pastor Squire Newsome
Greater Beulah Baptist Church

Darrick Johnson "Brother Malcolm",

Congratulations on taking time to share your journey, Darrick. It is one that is worthy of being told, and is made powerful by your willingness to work with your gift from the Creator: your resemblance to an American legend in Brother Minister Malcolm X. I have witnessed your personal journey of patience and commitment to being a father and husband, using the tools you have acquired along your path to continue to grow.

Thank you for being a shining example of Black Manhood!!!

Adeyemi Bandele,
Founder, Men on The Move

Dedication

Dedicated to the mothers and fathers of African Americans, kidnapped from their land, Mother Africa, cradle of all civilization. Fellow "human beings" forced to endure the inhumanity of being chained together, packed in the belly of a germ-infested slave ship. Forced to lie in the vomit of those who got sick during the months-long journey at sea. Forced to lie in their own urine and feces, as well as that of the others. An estimated fifteen percent of this human cargo—ranging from three hundred to more than four hundred people—died at sea. Bodies could easily be overlooked with so many people tightly chained together, and when discovered, they'd be thrown overboard. Sharks followed, looking to feast on human flesh.

Upon arrival to the new world, they were hosed down, auctioned off like cattle and forced to work from sunup to sundown. Then on Sunday, they were allowed a day off to go to church and sing about "freedom" when they died and went to heaven. Today, many are still being brainwashed in the name of religion.

All people stand upon the shoulders of the blood, sweat and tears of our African ancestors. Slavery—human trafficking—greatly assisted America in becoming the superpower that it is today, thanks to their sacrifice on behalf of us!

Life... it's not promised. Every day that we're breathing is a blessing. Upon coming to the conclusion of sharing my journey, I learned about the passing of a good friend, one whom I'd like to recognize, who assisted me in becoming a better playwright, poet, performer and person of creative genius: Joseph Briggs, aka, 1 Wise African. Strong personalities bumping heads, as was the case with us, is not always a bad thing. Joe challenged me on stage, encouraged me as a writer and was the first to introduce me as Brother Malcolm. If you knew Joe and his powerful, distinct voice, you know he made you step up or shut up. He was wise and wore the name African proudly. Physically gone, but brother, you will never be forgotten… R.I.P. my friend.

1 Wise African

Special thanks to my wife and best friend, Miss Cameo Johnson, who keeps me standing proudly upright and moving forward. If you know her, she's as sweet as can be, but on the other hand, Cam don't take no mess!

I'm reminded of many late nights, wee hours of the morning when she'd lift her head and say, "Darrick, turn off that computer. You need your rest. I need you here with me for a long time. Baby, we need each other…"

Thanks for always believing in me!

Introduction

When you hear the term Revolution, what comes to mind? Maybe war, protest, rebellion, the Civil—or rather, Human—Rights movement of the 1960s, overthrowing the government or even bloodshed, all of which can be aspects of it.

But actually, revolution is defined as making a drastic change. Like maybe changing the way we think in the hope of shifting consciousness and understanding the need to return to love, God's most powerful blessing!

Evolution is the biological process of change in all forms of life. It is evidence of growth and development—a theory based on the idea that all species are related and change over time. This is the core of evolution; without it, we'd all look and be the same.

I've come to understand the hardest times to go through in life are transitioning from one version of ourselves to another. However, it simply requires accepting who we are and allowing changes to occur naturally. Each of us goes through different tests, which can become unique mountaintop moments or challenges that make us feel deep in the valley of despair. You must roll with the punches of life and keep on pressing forward to make your life a masterpiece; imagine no limitations of what you can do or be.

Happiness depends upon the quality of your thoughts. Thoughts can become a habit—learned behaviors that can easily become automatic repetition, be it good or bad. So, guard accordingly. Gratitude is felt in acknowledging the quality of my own thoughts, in understanding the need to embrace my suffering to strengthen resiliency. Beneath anger, confusion and fear is an inner connection that leads us all to the basis of the source from which we all are created—Love, and God is.

Growing up in a dysfunctional family, I suffered the effects of mistrust, anxiety, depression and other negative emotions that could have easily led to me being a very insecure adult. Dysfunction rolls down from generation to generation, like a fire in the woods, taking down everything in its path. Until one person in one generation has the courage to face the flames to bring about inner peace and a true feeling of love. The truth that sets everyone free.

I've always been aware of the loving person deep within me, but when you don't feel it in return, love easily becomes anger. Psychology drew my interest as an adult who remembers as a young person constantly being called stupid by men in my family who were then unaware that they were nothing more than bullies. I learned in my studies that when you're ignored by the people whose attention means the most, the reaction in your brain is similar to that of physical pain.

So in order to embrace the love within, I had to first acknowledge the hurt and fear of the unknown. Doing so gave me a sense of comfort in being able to receive love and be loving, all while discovering my real strength had nothing to do with my physical state of being or how rapidly I could hit you with a 1, 3, 4, 3, 2 combination.

The dysfunction of my life has always been a fight. I was an angry, misdirected kid who felt love by giving the impression that I had no fear of fighting anyone, regardless of size. The transition from street fighter to boxer was fairly easy, therefore. I found joy in overcoming the odds when I found myself fighting someone twice my size, but faring pretty well. This built my confidence, despite still being lost, seeking but not yet finding direction.

My wife had taken notice, as did a family member who asked "Why every time you take a picture, you got your hands up in a tightly balled fist?"

As he speaks, my intensity rises. My cousin Jason has always had a way of getting inside my head, ever since we were kids—pushing my buttons. I take a deep breath and become silent, not as a sign of agreement but rather to remain calm. Despite being family and he a preacher, we both know that neither is going to back down. But we also know the deep-rooted love we share.

In answering the question from my wife and cousin, I realized that I had never paid attention until being asked. I took a moment to look through many pictures from the 1980s to now, and I did notice me always having a clenched fist. For the first time, I gave it some thought, and I came up with this:

It's my moral fortitude, my strength of character in doing what's right even when I may feel like doing wrong. Facing and withstanding adversity, always on guard, ready to defend the virtues representing the good that is me. Continually working to fully develop my purpose as a man of the people.

The fist doesn't define me; it simply represents a man of strength.

William Shakespeare wrote that the world is like a stage, and people are merely players. We all have exits and entrances, and one man in his time plays many parts.

We've all played various roles traveling through life. The roles we create in the process of being able to find and maintain peace require choosing to learn from life experiences. So with that said, I appreciate your interest in my journey. I hope sharing my story can assist in the quality of yours. We all have one—a story that describes our life's journey. The good, the bad, and yes, the ugly—which often for me was when a lack of preparation met reality.

Many of our behaviors are based on the type of environment in which we were reared. Borrowing a phrase from a friend, "My come-from place" has taught me that tough times don't last, but we certainly do. I am well aware of the lingering effects of the abusive environment where I grew up. I realize how it has played a role in my anxiety, depression and mood swings. Still, I've stood my ground and faced it head-on by pushing forward and lifting myself up, regardless of how I may feel at any given moment. I've learned to be gracious in recognizing that as long as I'm breathing, I know "everything gon' to be alright." I take on the responsibility to make today better than yesterday, and to God be the glory for giving me another opportunity to do so!

My early years were spent the same as a lot of kids: playing organized sports. Sports are a great character builder and are very beneficial in preparing our kids for life. As the oldest of my brother and sister, I always felt a lot of pressure along with feeling alone. Like most brothers, we were very competitive. I was a skinny little kid with an Afro as big as my body, but my little man complex drove my intensity.

I recall the lonely feelings of turning to look in the stands to see no one there cheering. Having someone cheer you on can be that boost of energy that's needed when your mind tries to convince you that you're dead-tired and giving up on myself added fuel to my anger and I turned to the self-medication of smoking weed and drinking alcohol.

I once read how all the crazy drama, tension and hostility frequently seen in people comes by way of family, most of who are unaware of the traumatic memories stored away in individual cells. These memories are passed on from generation to generation and this holds especially true in our African American culture where many of our experiences have been shaped during our fight for freedom, justice, equality and our God given rights to be respected and seen as fellow human beings.

I'm delighted to turn the page towards healing and discover the uniqueness of my journey. We've all unconsciously internalized certain unfavorable things by way of racism. It's an ugly history, perpetrated still by some in the so-called dominant culture.

This journey is about breaking the chains of cultural conditioning, set by them. Consider, like for instance, how boys are taught not to show emotions.

Both my brother and I started playing football at a young age;

he started at ten and I a year or so later, around age thirteen. The games were played on nearby fields, so when one team finished playing, we'd usually go over to cheer on the other team. When my game was over, with my parents absent as usual, my teammates and I would go over to the adjoining fields in support of the other teams. Right away, I'd hear and see both my parents, along with my father's brother, enthusiastically cheering on my brother. I'd submerge my feelings concerning their lack of interest in supporting me and ultimately do the same in cheering on Jeff 'Superman' Chapman. Despite my feelings 'that I didn't matter' I was so proud of my brother.

I eventually embraced the fact that he was a better all-around athlete. My pops and his brother—let me make it plain—were two mean mother fuckers who kept me on edge. Today, I have no shame in recognizing how their intimidation has led to my jumpiness, hands up in position, ready for combat when I get startled.

I recall a moment coming over to watch my brother's game after my own. I was walking up the stairs into the bleachers and came face to face with my uncle, who fiercely stared me up and down as if sizing me up to kick my ass. Suddenly I felt as if my huge afro shrunk in fear. He zoomed in on my cleats that had duct tape around the toes, holding together the cracked pleather. I don't recall his words, but trust me, they were fierce. However, such verbal attacks were nothing new. I recall how I use to frequently wake in a cold sweat after dreaming of kicking the ass of these grown-men.

Bullying is a learned behavior that emerges long before children step foot on campus. It has become a major problem in our country. Beating up and picking on people has transitioned into mass shootings. Hurt people hurt others who are hurting. But remember, when people say or do bad things to you, often it has nothing to do with you and everything to do with them. It's simply an indication of their insecurities with themselves (a learned behavior).

By way of God's grace, I've been able to make sense of my past and be at peace with it, while remaining in the process of developing my vision for tomorrow. I've been inspired by many voices, and they have broadened my mind and helped me find, feel and develop confidence in my own. Voices like that of my hero, Minister Malcolm X, who rose from the depths of prejudice, hate, poverty, crime and prison where he educated himself to become an elite intellectual who continues to influence even in death.

I recall reading about the revolutionary leader Ernesto "Che" Guevara, who said, "The true revolutionary is guided by a great feeling of love."

I also enjoy this quote from the legendary guitarist Jimi Hendrix: "When the power of love overcomes the love of power, the world will know peace."

I currently feel a greater sense of peace, embracing the love that is a part of me. My life has become less stressful because I chose to keep smiling; writing helps in leaving behind tensions to embrace joy and peace, to be happy.

Starting at a very young age, I developed a deep-rooted love and pride in my Blackness. I was a toddler in the 1960s, but when I'd see documentaries of the times, my attention was captured. I remember seeing John Calrose and Tommy Smith, two Olympic gold-medalists in track, as they stood on the podium and extended their black-gloved fists high into the sky during the playing of the national anthem to symbolize power to Black and oppressed people around the world. During the same 1968 Olympics, George Foreman just a few days later waved the American flag after winning a gold medal in boxing. He stated there was nothing political in his gesture, that he simply felt proud and then had to endure Black criticism. I make reference in reminding us to allow each other to be who we are, which makes us no less Black. I also remember Mr. Muhammad Ali, and not simply due to his greatness as a fighter. But rather his activism in refusing to go and fight in the Vietnam War and in his words, "Ain't no Vietcong ever called me nigger."

In 1988, I competed in the Eastern Olympic trials representing the U.S. Marines in boxing. I had a small red, black and green flag in my pocket that I wanted to wave alongside the small American they gave everyone for the opening ceremony. But I didn't have the courage to display it. I knew whites and maybe some Blacks would have lost their minds, and I wasn't equipped to handle it back then. Even today, when we stand and allow our voices to be heard according to the law, we are demonized, like Colin Kaepernick in 2016.

This journey is based on my truth—my development from my past of feeling as if I didn't even matter, to discovering my hidden truth of faith, commitment and dependability that is continually revealed. I'm much more patient, which is far more than waiting for something to happen. Rather, it is how you wait.

When I am tempted to lose patience, I stop and think about how patient God has been with me. So in looking back through the lenses of the former me, I'm happy to be continually unfolding. I'm not yet the man I desire to be, but grateful to be far removed from the man I once was. Living without fear, worry and doubt has helped expand my revolutionary spirit that is often met with societal resistance, but I am steadily learning not to react to.

Sometimes it only takes adjusting your attitude when faced with trying times.

The thoughts shared on the coming pages are me letting down my guard to expose my soul. My heart has chiseled through the rough outer shell that my journey has produced, the one well-versed in the toughness that molded the man I am. A man who now finds comfort in being gentler—or at least I try.

Fighting during my youth was like a rite of passage. It gave me a sense of significance rarely felt in my development from boy to man. Fear can cause a cowardly retreat or make you fight like a lion. I took pride in being king, all the while knowing who not to mess with. Fighting built my confidence, but it no longer describes or defines me. I've learned it's better to reveal so to heal as opposed to remaining stuck, always angered, potentially causing harm to myself or others. So it's my hope that I'm able to influence you to dream big and discover your full potential as I continue in the process of fully discovering my own. Sharing with you serves as a reminder to me on our ongoing journey of self-discovery, God gets the glory…

To be successful in struggle requires remembrance of the Creator and the doing of good deeds. This is important because struggle demands that there be a kind of social consciousness and a social commitment that joins Men together. - H. Rap Brown

CHAPTER 1

THE HEALING THERAPY IN WRITING

I've come to realize how writing has helped me discover myself, giving real insight into things that spark curiosity and build upon my strengths. This allows me to clearly articulate my thoughts and share feelings that help create what I desire.

Truth be told, I've lived much of my life uncertain of what that actually was. Before discovering the healing therapy of writing, I was lost. So much of my life has been spent only existing, whereas now I remain open to giving of myself in the hope of being a positive light in a world full of so much darkness.

Writing has helped me learn from negative experiences, and studies show that writing helps strengthen your immune system while it strengthens your mind. I now communicate more clearly. I have learned to eliminate stress while generating more productivity, along with an awareness that improves my decisions and helps me maintain focus. I've learned to measure success based on my own terms.

My love of writing came first from reading. Throughout my journey, I've been lifted by the joy I found in reading, which has helped me overcome some tough times!

Former President Harry S. Truman once stated: "In reading the lives of great men, I found that the first victory they won was over themselves... self-discipline with all of them came first."

Writing has broadened my vision and added enormous value to my soul, bringing me joy towards a higher level of consciousness. Some feelings are hard to verbalize, some thoughts still I don't quite understand, but I've found a way to manage those feelings through the self-expression of writing. Now I am truly enjoying my journey of self-discovery that writing continues to bring forth, and my efforts to enhance success have required a continued strengthening of my faith.

Most of my fights have been battles within, but writing continues to set me free.

No longer am I a prisoner inside my own mind, unconsciously mad at the world. Through writing, I've learned to better manage the angry Black man inside me. I'm clear about the world needing to return to love, with less hate, prejudice and bigotry, so that we as people can bring forth more understanding and heal humanity.

I began writing during the challenging times of starting a new chapter of my life, after the ending of a nine-year relationship that had produced two beautiful daughters.

I'm now clear that their mother suggesting I keep a journal was her way of saying, "Darrick, I will always love you, even if we are no longer in love."

Time taught me how pain and adversity evolve when you remain open, and the finger of blame never points in one direction. Blame can also be a great teacher that helps in moving us out of our own way. My ex-wife played a major role in awakening the sleeping giant within me, and her suffering in our failed union would make me better for the next woman.

But though the journal she brought me was a token of love, it was met with resistance. I recall my emotionally driven response: "I ain't keeping no damn diary." It was my way of trying to hide my broken heart.

So she strategically put it in my bag and stroked my ego in saying, "Darrick, you have so much to offer. Share your journey."

Still, I stood there as if on guard, trying to protect my shattered heart. So when she placed the journal in my possession, I said nothing and moved on.

Many lonely nights would follow, and one night I randomly picked up the journal and started putting pen to paper. I soon discovered how doing so kept me lifted, even spiritually enhanced, despite the loud sounds around me of drunken neighbors—men who occupied the other basement one-room apartments, men like me dealing with starting a new life after a breakup, after being kicked in the ass by love.

So began my daily practice that I called my conversations with God, who was well aware of my shattered heart. Still, his blessings come in abundance when we openly humble ourselves to receive his divine loving spirit. Writing simply started the process of my healing. Through it, I began to listen to God speak as the pen gave me answers, increasing my focus and faith along with a different type of courage, expanding beyond the physical that I had grown accustomed to while enhancing my critical thinking.

Being Black in America requires you to look below the surface by using your third eye. In one way or another, society is always trying to break us down, and by no means am I speaking self-pity as opposed to our Black reality.

I've learned throughout the course of my journey when to point the finger inward as opposed to out, to confront my own stuff with an open mind and loving spirit. This enables me to release any pent-up resistance that may be lingering and helps in being able to stand tall, like a leader.

There is nothing pleasant about a life full of stress. In fact, studies show that increased stress levels can lead to health issues that can ultimately kill, so either learn or die suffering. I grew tired of carrying the burden of pain. Challenges in life are unavoidable, but choosing to use tough times as a means to build enables me to expand my horizon towards higher levels of consciousness. I am continually learning to allow the challenges of life to teach as opposed to wear me down. I've grown strong enough to realize if I'm being driven by my E.G.O.—an acronym meaning Easing God Out—which means I'm bound to fail.

A real and effective leader first challenges the self. I'm reminded of how people can play an influential role in our development or demise. I recall working under the supervision of proud Army veteran Mr. Clarence Frazier, a man who was easygoing like Sunday morning and who often had a story to go along with his warm spirit. Through him, I learned the significance of listening. His stories were often long and drawn out, but I'd maintain patience, trying not to interrupt. Instead, I would listen and carefully consume what he was sharing. Usually, at the end of his mini-sermon, I'd be left with what Ms. Oprah Winfrey calls those 'Aha' moments. He's a man who I occasionally still turn to for insight.

Mr. Clarence and I shared many life lessons, many laughs and disappointments during the years we worked together. At the time, I had an aggressive nature. There were times that my emotions ran high and would sometimes get ahead of my intellect. When things settled down, Mr. Clarence would often come over to my still raging self to say, "Darrick, you must allow people to be who they are, and then ask yourself the motive behind your actions."

Often, I didn't want to hear it, but he made me think. I'd be reminded of my youth as an angry young man who lacked any real direction, struggling to find myself while trying to balance the emotional chaos that was me! Gratitude is felt in recognizing how our experiences help make sense of the past, bringing peace today and creating visions for tomorrow.

I'll never forget one particular day as a fifteen-year-old in 1978. I was skipping class, hanging out in my school's library, lounging and contemplating my next move—which was likely where I could dip and smoke another joint. I was a pothead during my school days, and smoking weed played a significant role in my struggles throughout. Suddenly, I felt as if I was being watched, so I displayed some early skills in acting as if looking for a particular book. I reached down and randomly picked one up.

The teacher came my way to investigate me, the young man who had spent more time in the principal's office than the library. I dramatically started flipping through pages, when suddenly my attention was captured. Now I was no longer faking, but rather fully engaged, reading the captions under the pictures of Minister Malcolm X in a small pictorial book entitled *The Life and Times of Malcolm X*.

I'm certain I had heard the name before then, because anything or anybody engaged in Black culture captured my attention, even as a very young man. Right away, I felt a sense of excitement reading each caption. I started to feel a connection to his look of intensity, standing behind a podium looking strong and stern like he was really saying something of significance.

Soon, I was no longer faking reading the book. The bell rang to indicate the end of class, and I slipped the book into my bookbag. I wanted to read more, but was too lazy to check the book out like I was supposed to do. It was the first book that I read on my own, having no idea of its significance in my life.

The military can be a good start in gaining direction in your life. It certainly did so for me, but not in the way that some may think. I was influenced by others who were more informed about many things than me, which was influential in wanting to read more. I was in my fourth of a six-year commitment to duty when I realized that the military wasn't for me, but I cherish the many wonderful people I met from different parts of the country. Being the old soul that I am, I usually connected with those who were older and more mature, with a higher level of consciousness that would have a great impact on me.

This brings to mind the saying that, if you're the smartest one of the group you hang with, you need new friends.

The brothers I'd meet while stationed in Okinawa, Japan, turned me onto activist and poet Haki Madhubuti, who ran a Black publishing company. I started ordering books and soon discovered a newfound joy in reading. I read books by former pimp turned author Iceberg Slim, who wrote about hustling, pimping and getting one over on the man, and books by Donald Goins.

As my mind became more engaged, I looked for books with better content, such as *Bloods, Black Veterans of the Vietnam War* by William Terry. I read other books about Blacks fighting for America's freedom, only to return home and see that Black people still weren't free. I recalled seeing protests against the war in Vietnam, and Mr. Muhammad Ali's defiance in refusing to go. Little did I know then that my purpose was being nurtured.

I'd go on to read several books about our Black struggle. The most influential would be Alex Haley's *Autobiography of Malcolm X*, which I borrowed from my school over and over. These books had a significant impact on me, and today I have adopted the practice of regularly reading something of spiritual or intellectual substance nearly every day. I've been influenced by great thinkers past and present, and for many who have come to know me over the years, it should come to no surprise that Minister Malcolm X and his influence on me stands out amongst the rest. His life helped me recognize that regardless of your past, you have the power to overcome adversity. Malcolm once described this as having the potential to be your greatest teacher.

I've learned that the first step in ridding yourself of a problem is acknowledgment. So my rough edges come naturally, and I do my best to bring a sense of calm to deal with my sometimes stern, aggressive nature and my nervous energy. Writing has helped me tremendously, and I am a much-improved person.

Despite his hard edge, my father who raised me was a loving man. But he didn't know how to show what was on the inside to me, the boy he was raising.

The male ego can be a powerful force, especially after drinking, and my father did plenty of that. I feel certain that he and my biological dad crossed paths a number of times, based on their mutual interest in drag racing. And when under the influence, the mind can wander, causing one to take out frustrations and resentment on innocent victims—remember me speaking of when the ego leads? I speculate that frustrations were taken out on me, the boy he was raising, who strongly resembled his biological father.

My earliest memory of being told that I wasn't family occurred around age eleven, and how I was told certainly wasn't pleasant. Instead, it was spoken in a harsh, demeaning manner in response to something I did or didn't do that wasn't up to his approval: "You sure ain't no Chapman." I'd hear the same coming from his brother, who in my early years was our neighbor. I often felt like a trembling lamb between two hungry wolves.

Fast forward, it was certainly unexpected when my pops who raised me acknowledged the death of my biological father, John Bug Marshal, who transitioned in the year 2011. He looked to me and said, "Darrick, I am sorry about the loss of your father." I don't think he was ever certain about whether my biological father and I had ever established a relationship—we hadn't. He'd have these big parties that I'd attend. We'd acknowledge one another and then be gone partying. Actually, I felt that I learned more about him a week or so before his death as we sat together in his living room, quietly examining each other.

Two years later, in April of 2013, George W. Chapman, who raised me, transitioned after lying in a coma for nearly two years. I would often go sit with and talk to his lifeless former self, wondering if he could understand me. After many conversations between my mom, brother and sister, we decided it was time to take him off the breathing machine and allow him to transition into his next phase of the hereafter.

Today I see remnants of both my fathers in me, knowing that their spirits look down with a sense of pride concerning the man that I've become.

I'm reminded of the saying of how God provides what we need, when we need it. Writing wasn't the only tool that helped me grow; I was also heavily involved with community and spirit-based groups that helped me learn to use life's difficulties as teachable moments. They helped me realize that fear and intimidation are an emotional hindrance. I suffered from both, but to God be the glory that I continue to demonstrate once again that tough times don't last, but we do!

I don't recall many dreams of what I wanted to be in my future.

Anger festered, so I was always fighting and my intensity only grew. I served in the Marines under the name of Chapman, which wasn't on my birth certificate or driver's license. Rather, I told the recruiter that I went by Chapman. Looking back, I realize these recruiters are only trying to reach quotas, so if you say it's your name, it is, and just sign the dotted line.

When I got out of the military, my veteran status got me a job in the Federal Government under Chapman, and no longer having a military I.D. caused a problem. I recall sharing my dilemma with my uncle, who got me the job. He's the same one who intimidated me back when I was younger.

He said, "You should have taken care of that a long time ago!"

I thought to myself, "I should have never been put in such a position of being lied to in the first place."

So, to make things simple, in the year 1991, I decided to be known by my name given at birth: Darrick A. Johnson, as opposed to the name given when my mother married in 1965. The change was also made after my former wife said to me, "Who am I going to be, Mrs. Chapman or Johnson?"

Mentally and emotionally, I was enduring some tough times, feeling a lack of identity. It took a minute for some people to get used to calling me D.J. as opposed to D.C. It was especially rough after getting married in 1992, and all the teasing of, "Damn, D. I thought the woman changed her last name, not the man."

Memories of my traumatic childhood moved me towards my purpose of being a difference-maker, who now can show love, be loving and love my current state of being. As children, we blossom into young adults who mimic that which we see displayed around us, and the vast majority of what I recall seeing was a bunch of profanity-laced anger and intimidation. All of which contributed to my aggressive energy. And as I grew older, my fuse grew shorter—especially when under the influence of alcohol.

I was around twelve when I first experimented with drinking.

Pops always had cold Budweiser left in his cooler that he'd place in the garage after getting home from his job as a construction worker. This was around the same time that I started smoking weed. Being a child born in the early 1960s meant coming of age during the disco and funk era of the 1970s. A time when life simply went up in smoke, in reference to a popular Cheech and Chong movie in the late 1970s that many of us found hilarious because we, too, enjoyed taking two pulls and pass so that the joint could last.

There was always the discussion when we were high about weed being natural, so why is it illegal to use? We'd then begin to feel we were getting deep and intellectual in our discussion. But getting high on weed made me more relaxed and less nervous. My free spirit would explore like an eagle, a "Black Eagle" gliding high across the sky.

I often joke about the many years of smoking weed one minute and getting banged upside the head the next in a boxing ring, knowing that many brain cells were killed as I frequently engaged in both. But at least getting high made me mellow as opposed to angry or aggressive, which was the case when I drank excessively. Then I would be ready to fight at any moment for the slightest of infractions, getting hot for basically not being able to take a joke.

I recall as a teen feeling guilty about being a bully, but I now recognize that I was simply acting out that which was done to me by my father, his brother and even my grandfather. I now equate my feeling of guilt in taking advantage of weaker people as God speaking through me at a very early age. Now, I remain on a more spiritual path in my efforts to build a stronger relationship between God and me.

I learned a very valuable lesson from my former wife. She'd see me get mad when the other person may have been joking, and she'd say, "Stop allowing people to get inside your head."

We live and learn, and today I try to not be rattled by another's words. In focusing on the now, I know that I've become a much better person. I believe in the universal principle of whatever energy you release will eventually be brought back to you. A night of dancing, a passion of mine, would ultimately bring me love.

I recall just before remarrying in 2011, the two sisters who facilitated a spiritual group I had joined expressed their happiness for me after meeting my wife-to-be. I recall getting somewhat offended when one of the sisters said, "I'm happy to see that you have finally gotten over your former wife."

I debated and denied her accusations, then finally came to grips with her point of view. In looking back through the rearview mirror of life, I've gained a greater insight, and I will continue moving forward on the roads less traveled, discovering new things about me and myself.

I am a man who now finds comfort in the warmth of my smile and being able to exist in a state of joy, peace and doing my best to spread love. The intensity remains, but I feel well balanced.

After completing my military service, I engaged in community outreach. My fairly new interest in reading led me to a Writing for Healing workshop and an everlasting friendship with a woman whom I still confide in for advice. We have our differences, but not only do opposites attract, they're also the best to learn from. Recognizing this value has helped us remain friends.

I recall an assignment that required us to describe what was referred to as our "come-from place" using our five senses—sight, smell, taste, hearing and touch. This helped me to better articulate deep-rooted feelings and emotions that often kept me from being in touch with myself. I soon recognized that I was still hurting and craving love, while not quite understanding how to love myself.

In time, my confidence increased and became more real as opposed to a mask of a bold demeanor. I knew nothing about poetry, but one day I just stepped to the mic and began to express my raw feelings. I called it poetry, but I certainly wasn't well established. So when I was chosen by this female friend as one of the facilitating poets to host an event called Conversation Poetry, truth be told, I kind of felt that my selection was more her digging on me as opposed to my skills as a poet. But as mentioned, I've always been bold, so no lack of confidence would stop me from participating. In looking back, it was a job well done and I was a proud participant.

There were five or six of us who would agree upon a subject to poetically speak on in order to lead the audience into meaningful conversation. After one of our many successful nights, we all headed to a friend's house for drinks. Before you know it, it's late and everyone is twisted.

The host suggests we all spend the night instead of getting behind the wheel to drive, and she gets blankets. I'm busy creating a space on the sofa, when she abruptly points to me and says, "No, you're coming with me."

That drew woahs from everyone. Two fellas were present, and they gave me a look of "What you gon' do, bra?"

My mind immediately said no, I'm not interested, but ego lifted me from the sofa and got my feet walking up the stairs. Because I wasn't strong enough to simply say "No" to her advances, I ended up going through with the act with not much enjoyment.

I was reminded of a lesson learned from my former wife, who would say that making love starts in the mind. The body operates in accordance with what the mind is speaking, and I had been led by my ego because I was called out on the spot.

I remember the conversations we had afterward, and I was very honest. I explained how she'd put me on the spot and that I was not physically attracted. That it was my ego and not desire that cause me to respond to her advances. I told her having casual sex with someone where no physical attraction existed was not my desire, and I worried this could ruin our friendship.

One thing that I didn't say—and which was also true—was, "Hey, I know me, and no matter how much I try, my lack of desire would eventually bring the ugly out of me, and I'm certain this would not have been appreciated."

Afterward, I felt a sense of pride in my honesty and maturity. I had grown to no longer want to have sex with a woman simply because it was available.

I continue to discover new things about me through writing and its healing therapy. God's grace has enabled me to chisel away at some of my bad traits and behaviors that occasionally flare up, and I can make the necessary adjustments to come back into a kind, loving nature.

CHAPTER 2

MENTAL STABILITY

Nearly one in five adults in the United States currently lives with a mental health disorder, and I continue to work on my own mental and emotional stability. I've encountered bouts of depression, anxiety, irritability, and mood swings that have taken me high and low, and there is no shame in recognition.

We all experience our share of highs and lows throughout the journey called life, and our ability to handle the many tests that life presents is a measure of strength of character. When you pay attention, you'll recognize that life is as unpredictable as an earthquake and as beautiful as spring. There's an old proverb that reads, "Smooth seas do not make skillful sailors." We don't grow when things come easy.

Being dumped proved to be a hard pill to swallow, and whoever said a man doesn't cry didn't see the tears running down my face. Through blurred vision, I reached down to retrieve the pieces of my shattered heart, but I refused to allow myself to fall victim by feeling sorry for myself. I pulled myself up by my bootstraps, so to begin a new life as a single father.

I quickly developed a greater sense of clarity and began to face the pain by articulating my thoughts through writing, which helped me to better understand what I truly felt. Some things made me point my finger inwards, so to deal with my part in whatever the problem. I am now quite clear that I did not love enough of me. I continued the practice of writing daily, and I began to feel stronger as I started to refer to my journaling as my personal conversations with God. By way of meditation, I was able to hear God speak.

I learned the hard way, as I normally do, that words can hurt just as bad as those sticks and stones. I had called my former wife "Bitch" for the umpteenth time. This finally drove her to grab a steak knife and cut me across my shoulder. It took everything in me to move beyond the emotional impulse of responding to her physical violence with my own by going upside her head.

I was momentarily struck with disbelief as blood streamed across my chest, followed by tears of hurt and rage. But everything froze when I noticed our baby girl had been awakened by all the commotion from her parents. She looked confused, coming out of her bedroom to see her dad bleeding with tears streaming down my face. Right then, I refused to be provoked into stooping below the standards I had set for myself as a young man.

I had grown up seeing what I was now caught up in the middle of many times before. I vowed never to put my hands on a woman. Although for a split second, I was feeling justified in defending myself—or rather kicking her ass—in response to her cutting me, no question in my mind had I slugged her, all hell would have broken loose. She would have fought me, and the experience would have become much uglier.

It was tough walking away, and it made me feel like a punk. But in reflecting back to this ugly moment, I am glad that I was able to stop myself, take a deep breath and settle down my raging emotions. That allowed me to think critically after seeing that our youngest daughter had witnessed this ugly commotion between her parents—an ugliness that I knew all too well. But with balanced emotions, I gained control and did not emotionally respond.

I can be violent, but my nature is not.

This burden was on my mind for years, but I came to realize that it wasn't my burden to carry alone: "Cast your burden on the Lord, and He shall sustain you; He shall never permit the righteous to be moved." (Psalm 55:22)

I eventually learned to release it and let go by affirming the beauty, strength and stability of me. Not long after my separation, I found refuge at Inner Visions Spiritual Life, where I discovered the significance of affirmations to affirm my absolute best: "Nothing happens to you, but rather for you when you see the positive even in the negative events of life, remain open and learn the lesson." Joel Osteen.

I'm still winning the battle against depression that occasionally tries to flare up, but my mental and emotional stability has grown stronger, and I've developed the willpower to defeat depression. After months of living in a room in the basement of someone's home followed by a year of rooming with the younger brother of my best friend, who had transitioned a year or so prior I'd taken up residency in Washington, D.C. for the next eleven years to start my new beginnings.

I recall how my conversations with God through writing made me feel empowered after being kicked in the ass—or rather, to the curb—by love. I quickly grew tired of the same old routine of drowning my sorrows in the bottle, joined by a bunch of drunken fools trying to convince each other in being justified in pointing the finger of blame outward as opposed to looking within. Drinking all their blues away, along with the occasional scream of, "Da Bitch ain't shit!"

But my conversations by way of writing helped to make sense of the dysfunctional mess that was partially due to me. Eventually, I learned to eject instead of replaying the tape of agony over and over inside my mind, retelling the stories with an unconscious hope of validating my assessment concerning whatever failure I was going through.

I continued to write, and introduced the world to the new and improved Darrick.

My former wife was absolutely right in making me better for

the next woman, to whom I am happily married today. I am pleased to see that my former and current wife get along well when in each other's presence. Our children were eighteen and twenty-four when I remarried, and I recall confiding in them so to get a feel of how they felt in me remarrying. The answer is clear, and I'm certain this plays a role in the good relationship between my former and current wife.

The lesson learned is that some people come into your life for a season as opposed to a lifetime. My first wife suggesting that I write caused me to look within myself, and these conversations with God became words of healing. I would ultimately spend more time in prayer, meditation and being still, which helped me to push through all the muck of hurt, sorrow and rejection that tried convincing me that I was a failure.

I had my moments of dwelling on things that hadn't gone so well. For instance, my failures in school, which in turn caused men in my family to bombard me with insults of being stupid. Back then, all I could do was feel helpless, filled with a rage that churned within and further hardened my outer shell. That was followed by my military difficulties and a host of other things, all trying to convince me that no one had any real expectations of me achieving much of anything. But instead, these negative words became my motivation.

I recall hearing echoes whenever things weren't going so well of my pops saying to my mother when she finally decided that she had enough of his abusive ways. "Go ahead, leave! You'll be back, because that nigger there will be dead or in jail!

Hurtful words that influenced me not to fail!

So regardless of whatever situation I found myself in, I'd find a way out and push through depression. I'd stake claim that no permanent space of doubt will remain within me. Writing served as my tool to boost my confidence and ultimately made me better. I still have several journals that I sometimes read to remind me where I came from and the work that still needs to be done.

The practice of writing is the driving force that keeps renewing the creative spirit that was always there. I recall when I began to notice the way my words would flow. The pain from the divorce was starting to fade and I was slowly adjusting to my new life as a single dad. My weekends were always reserved for my daughters Diamond and Jasmine, and it was their sugar and spice that made me become more open and nicer.

Another transition before the breakup was me finally walking away from my first love of boxing, and my girls played a major role in this decision. Their mother's work schedule required me to take my girls to the boxing gym with me, and the girls had seen me in tough scraps before, where I may have received a bloody nose or a black eye. But on this day, they watched me having to pull myself up from the canvas on two occasions. I saw his punches coming, but my reaction wasn't quick enough to avoid getting hit—and this sucka hit hard. I'd learn when Father Time sinks in, the first thing you lose is timing.

After stepping out of the ring, I noticed my baby girl Diamond, who was somewhere around four at the time. Her eyes were watery, and I kneeled down before her.

"Daddy," she said, "I don't want to see you get hit anymore."

My heart melted as I embraced her, still wearing my boxing gloves. I reassured her that I was alright.

"But Daddy, I don't like seeing you get hit," Diamond said. Jasmine's concerns were echoed on her face.

The girls had seen me get hit many times—they practically grew up around boxing—but they had never seen me take the type of punishment that sent me down to the canvas twice that day. So in the next few days, I did some serious soul searching.

I was living multiple lives as a hard-working, truck-driving warehouse worker, dedicated father and fighter, who also suffered from depression that I treated by drinking heavily and smoking weed. I finally came to my senses in realizing that there was a good chance of me getting seriously hurt if I continued to live in such a way.

I had been in and out of the gym, battling increasing depression as my divorce lingered, but I was forced to face the logic. We were better simply being the best parent that we could be as opposed to being a married couple. It was tough going through it, but in looking back, our separation was best.

Despite the painful backstory, ours is a positive example of Black love.

As mentioned, my former and current wife get along well. My former wife's new partner, Larry, and I are real cool as well, Jasmine's my oldest daughter's biological father Reginald and I get along well.

A moment that I'm proud of is when Diamond graduated college. In the years following the separation between their mother and me, they would tell me Larry was a good guy. I didn't want to like him, because I was hurting, but everything must run its course—a lesson learned in First Sunday. At Diamond's graduation, Larry comes to congratulate me.

I turned to him and said, "Congratulations to you as well, my brother. You were the one that my girls turned to throughout the week. They've always spoken highly of you, so congratulations for a job well done as well."

I felt really good afterwards and said to myself, "This is the way it needs to be done. Breakups happen, but we still need to be parents—which includes accepting the other person coming into their life."

I've made many references to reading, but it was not my only source of information.

After returning home to the States after a year of duty in Japan, I discovered WOL-AM 1450, Where Information Is Power. Back then, the founder of Radio One, Ms. Kathy Hughes herself, was on the air, as the station was in the process of growing. As a truck driver, I was always tuned in, enjoying the various hosts who came and went over the years, many of whom I built relationships with. I listened religiously and became a frequent caller, who was also featured on the airwaves through my poetry and community service.

It was on the airwaves that I first met a writer who I'd later befriend: Mr. Jose Villegas III. He was promoting his book, *Emotional* **Prisoner**

(Trapped Behind the Bars of My Thoughts), and it truly inspired me. I could relate to the title alone, and after reading it—along with other books about mental health—I noticed how many of the symptoms I was reading about spoke to me.

I recall my first visit to a therapist. It turned me off, because she was so quick to prescribe medication. She warned about the possibility of suicidal thoughts, and I quickly replied, "Whoa, that's okay. I don't need or want any drugs to make me consider suicide any further than I already have." My faith, will, and continued study have been strong enough to push me through such thoughts and deal with my bouts of depression.

Mental health disorders are a real issue in our community, and we must move beyond the stigma of being seen as crazy or being weak. After hearing Jose on the radio, I went to his book signing and purchased a copy. He and I connected fairly well, and he inspired in me the need to tell my own story. As I mentioned in the beginning, we all have one, but the determining factor of the quality of your life story is based on the choices you make.

I currently reside in a space where I choose me.

Over the years, I've been moved by several authors and spoken-word artists who continue to encourage me. Writing has built an inner strength that I had never felt before, not even as a fighter. Although far removed from competing, I still crave to get back in the ring. I'll always be a fighter, one who pushes through whatever the obstacle, even my own self-inflicted wounds. I've gotten much better in recognizing whether I am emotionally driven as opposed to being mentally focused in order to learn from my transgression. That tool has been placed in my fix-it box to retrieve whenever needed. I'm listening, writing and learning as I remain open in the process on the road towards discovery!

I recall the bright, sunny, spring-like day in the late 1990s. I was out on the road doing my job as a delivery truck driver, killing time by exploring downtown, when the name of a building captured my attention.

The Inner Visions Spiritual Life Center

I parked the van and followed my thoughts as I ventured through the doors, where I was greeted warmly by two women who I'd learn were sisters. They informed me that the center was run by a woman who I vaguely recall hearing about or maybe even seeing on the Oprah Winfrey show, Ms. Iyanla Vanzant. She wasn't there on this particular day, but I would go on to meet and get to know her. Her book *The Spirit of a Man* was one of the first I'd read in my quest to learn more about how to build my relationship with God.

I've always possessed a deep-rooted love and pride in my Blackness, and that cultural presence was felt there at Inner Visions. I recall sharing this experience with some of my family, so-called Christians who gave the assumption that I must be affiliated with the Nation of Islam (N.O.I.). This is by no means is a slight against my many colleagues and associates in the nation, but I find it quite interesting how "some" make it seem as if taking pride in your Blackness is unconventional. As if only members of the N.O.I. are allowed such pride.

I'm reminded of a James Baldwin quote: "To be a Negro in this country and to be relatively conscious is to be in a rage almost all the time."

Thinking back to the men I saw growing up, it appeared that they were always angry—a description on occasions I'd hear about me, looking as if I were mad at the world.

My youngest daughter, who was somewhere around nine years old at the time, once said to me, "Daddy, why do old people always look so mean?"

I wonder sometimes, does this question now apply to me?

I remember walking into my grandmother's home and being greeted by a statue of a blonde-haired, blue-eyed Jesus. I view that as the ultimate mental conditioning of inferiority. Does it not say in the Ten Commandments that "Thou shalt not make unto thee any graven image or any likeness of anything that is in heaven above, or that is in the earth beneath."

My developing sense of awareness was being unconsciously challenged as I was force-fed religion by my family. I ultimately built up the courage to express my discomfort during one of our family's annual Sunday soul food dinners. This moment reminds me of an episode of *Good Times*, the popular T.V. sitcom of the 1970s, in which J.J. was painting an image of Jesus being Black. Michael, his militant little brother, was excited about J.J.'s more accurate description according to scripture, while Miss Evans nearly lost her mind, unaware of how this false image was made to make us feel less than equal in an unjust America.

When I made my comment, I remember being nervous as opposed to my fantasy of speaking with the boldness and authority of Malcolm X in the Spike Lee movie when he challenged a White priest about the color of Jesus.

My uncle said, "Well, I don't need anyone convincing me to be proud to be Black."

I replied in a cracked, mumbled voice, "Neither do I. But what I see in this statue and the many depictions of Jesus certainly don't match the description in Revelations. And if there aren't supposed to be any images of him, why does the bible give a description?"

I strongly feel that we've allowed religion, which is supposed to be a personal relationship between an individual and God, to divide us. Regardless of what you believe in, all religions have the same common purpose of getting you closer to your source. No person is going to get you into heaven, so why is so much energy wasted in being concerned about what another believes is right or wrong, if they're not hurting anyone?

We're all made in His image.

CHAPTER 3

WE ALL WEAR THE MASK; IT'S NEITHER GOOD NOR BAD!

Alright, let me make it plain! People act and do things differently when they think someone is watching. I equate this to wearing a mask. We hide aspects of who we really are. However, much of the real person seldom changes. The mask is usually in the form of what we want people to see.

I myself have often worn the mask, trying to shield and cover mean and nasty aspects of me that sometimes make their way to the surface, especially when I was drinking.

Ask any vet how the military unconsciously promotes alcoholism. Bars, or what my father used to call beer gardens, are everywhere on and around bases. I recall when stationed overseas having a beer machine in our barracks, and the cost of buying one in 1986 when stationed in Okinawa, Japan was maybe a dollar. Everyone had some sort of liquor stash in their locker, so after our final formation, the bottle would be passed around, before heading out to the N.C.O. Club and more alcohol.

The Air Force bases, who had the best of everything—especially women—restricted Marines from their clubs due to our tendency of getting drunk and fighting. I recall protesting this policy, getting myself and friends in, only to turn and be a big old hypocrite by allowing someone to rub me the wrong way. Soon I'd be fighting, because my fuse was short and I was easily triggered. But when things calmed down, I donned the mask—bringing forth my charm. And I'd eventually talk my way into being let back in. Through God's grace, I'm here to talk about it. Sadly, in the world we live today, I would have likely caught a bullet by now!

It got to a point with me where guys would say, "There's Chap, he going to fight tonight." I was quick to provoke trouble, and this kept me in trouble and hindered my forward progress as a U.S. Marine.

I recall during boot camp and military occupational school often being chosen to lead, but there was something within me that could not submit to the Marine Corps' way of doing things. I've always been disciplined, but also rebellious. It's the way that I was raised, and there was no drill instructor tougher than my father, George W. Chapman.

I realize my father also wore the mask. He was a loving, good-spirited man, but when under the influence, his demons emerged. I hear my mother say, "Boy, you know the apple doesn't fall very far from the tree…"

I've always been a charming person, but I've also known how to wear the mask to cover the mean-spirited side of me. Today, I am grateful to be more in control of the mean and nasty, as opposed to allowing it control over me. I am well aware of how alcohol often brought forth my ugly, and I can hear my wife saying, "Nasty hasn't gone anywhere; it's always near and can still flare up."

I know this, and I remain work in progress. I am more in touch with myself, and I don't wear the mask much anymore, grateful to be far removed from the man I once was. My current state of awareness and maturity has helped me develop a better understanding of myself and be aware of my inner rage that I've learned to channel in more constructive ways.

Mental health issues in our community are very real, and I myself have suffered from bipolar disorder, also referred to as manic depression. Some who have been closest to me are well aware of my mood swings, and likely pleased to hear me admit to having these issues that have gotten much better.

No longer do I take it personally when being teased about what I already knew about myself. Reading and study have helped me to become better equipped in dealing with my mood swings.

None of us are perfect; only God has that distinction. So remove your mask, pray, meditate, maintain faith and seek God's perfection as best you can.

Look closely at yourself in an attempt to bring forth your very best. I'm still in the process of removing the mask and facing my contradictions, so to allow my loving nature to shine bright without fear of what people think. Let's recognize the good in each other; we all know life can be difficult, and it rubs each of us in different ways. My recognition of using the mask to try to cover my flaws has caused me to dig deep and face whatever consequences may arise—being proactive instead of reactive.

Fear is simply a reaction to an anticipated danger, so I encourage you to stand tall and face whatever arises. Repeat inside your mind, "Tough times don't last, but we do!" I encourage you to work on improving yourself the same way you might develop muscles through exercise. You can exercise your mind by reading regularly and incorporating prayer and meditation into your life. So let's stay the course together.

My life has mainly been focused on the well-being of Black men—in particular being one myself—but I have a concern for all Men that God ordained with the responsibility to lead. Within us, the Black man in America, there lies an historic oppression that we must face in constructive ways.

I remember a book that was one of the first to lead me on my current spiritual journey. I was able to move beyond the book's distorted cover, which displayed a picture of a blond, blue-eyed Jesus. I recall ultimately saying to myself that, if all of these spiritual, afro-centric teachers I had grown to admire at Inner Visions were themselves always quoting the book, there must be something to it.

The title of the book was *Love Without Conditions: Reflections of the Christ Mind* by Paul Ferrini, whom I had met at Inner Visions. In it was a quote I remember: "Life is either resistance or surrender; there only two choices, one leads to suffering while the other leads to bliss. Resistance is the decision to act alone, while surrender is the decision to act with God. You cannot experience joy by opposing others; you can only experience it by remaining faithful to the truth within your own heart and my heart remains open." - Joyce Myers

Contrary to belief, we're all different in our opinions about Black diversity. Many choose to forget the horrors of the Black experience, fearing anger, while others like me choose to embrace and learn in the hope of healing humanity. I've discovered during my journey that the difficult moments that we all experience in life leave us with the choice to either remain stuck, dwelling in disappointment, or use whatever the challenge as a building block to manifest growth. Failure only occurs if you quit, and the words we choose to use during difficult moments can make a big difference.

Changing the way we interpret the challenge enables us to be more successful the next time around and moves us towards a higher level of consciousness. Over the years, I've learned that the words we choose to use can either encourage or cripple, a lesson learned firsthand. I'm sure most recognize the importance of this. We've all heard the old saying of how we live and learn. Life is beautiful, and the challenges we face in it often leave scars, but it's all a part of the process of getting better.

So remain faithful and know that those scars are reminders of God's mercy—and some are self-inflicted wounds. Keep yourself mindful of the various masks that we all wear. They are not necessarily good or bad, but rather prepare you to handle situations with kindness and consideration, which in turn helps make our world better!

CHAPTER 4

STRONG PEOPLE DON'T SHOW STRENGTH IN FRONT OF US RATHER, IT'S SHOWN BY THOSE WHO WIN BATTLES MOST KNOW NOTHING ABOUT.

Scientists have long demonstrated that hurtful words and intimidation from adults have tremendous negative effects on a child's development. I learned fairly quickly that sticks and stones can break your bones, but words do hurt as well. They can break us down, especially when coming from those we love and who claim to love us.

A boy wants nothing more than to please his father, and when he feels unable to gain his approval, anger begins to build. I was bombarded with insults from a young age, bullied by so-called, grown-ass men. And as I was accused of being slow and stupid, humiliation and anger took hold. I developed the feeling of no one believing in me, which made it hard to believe in myself.

As a young teen, I remember one of my father's friends, whose son had a slight mental challenge. I used to pick on him, and in time I came to realize that I was simply acting out what was being done to me. Picking on someone weaker is usually a sign of the bully's insecurity.

In looking back, I would say to young Darrick, "You're on the right path. Remain open and be that door for others to walk through. Know that no matter what, you can make it."

My fight was to just keep on pushing, knowing that the burden was not mine to bear alone. Jesus had already done so for you-me-us! In all my years as a boxer, where I won as many as I lost, it wasn't consistency in the ring that was needed as opposed to consistency in my life. I needed to remain focused on me, pushing through all the negativity inside my head. I needed to understand that people make conclusions based on what they think as opposed to what is known. I was lost, feeling alone, but not trusting or believing in anyone.

However, I was clear about my toughness—which ultimately made me believe in me.

Getting hurt is as natural as breathing, and overcoming hurt allows you to recognize your own strength. In time, I was able to recognize the need to be in control of my destiny, which took learning how to remain in control of my temper. I learned to stop being so reactionary, and instead take a deep breath, pause, and determine if there's a need to respond. I learned to separate my feelings while assessing the situation, and more often than not, I was able to choose to show compassion with a keen awareness of the suffering of another—having been in the space of pain, chaos and confusion many times myself.

I've always been aware of the good that is me, despite not always displaying it. The practice of deep breathing, prayer and meditation has helped me counter the negative with positive and see obstacles as opportunities. I no longer match anger with anger.

Maya Angelou states: "Do the best you can until you know better.

Then when you know better, do better."

Everything in life is learned behavior, and the worst person to be around is someone who complains about everything and appreciates nothing. I recall once being that person, but I made a choice to leave him in my past. I know now how emotional pain often starts at home, perpetrated by those who are closest and who haven't learned how to deal with their own mental and emotional instability. Sadly, it's a continual cycle that too often results in bullying. I believe that more attention needs to be generated towards the bully to help understand their reasons, in order to break the cycle.

As a bully in recovery, one who is better in control of my emotions instead of being driven by them, I can say it takes a conscious effort to break the chains of learned behavior. I recall being told that I wasn't doing something right, not good enough, ain't worth a damn, followed by, "You sho ain't one of us." I think most can understand how this could play on a boy's physiological well-being.

I recall the many times wishing I could crawl inside myself or go unnoticed. I'd easily fall victim to others who were joking or just clowning around because I was unable to take being the butt of the joke. A fellow Marine in my unit from Georgia who was fun-loving and quick-witted, with a very sharp sarcastic tongue, once punctured a wound in calling me "dummy," mimicking a deaf and dumb man who was being falsely accused of murder in the 1979 movie *Dummy*.

I was boiling with rage trying to keep my composure, despite feeling humiliated. In contrast, he saw it as just having fun—a classic example of the insensitivity shown to fellow human beings. I wanted so badly to punch him out, but was well aware of how I was already hanging on a very thin branch during this phase of military service. I was mad as hell, but able to walk away. The memory lingered long after it had been said and done, even when it appeared things between he and I had been settled. But as mentioned, he saw it as joking around, whereas I took it very seriously.

I could share many similar stories, where the other person was joking as I was hurting. But eventually, I'd feel guilt responding in anger, and this caused me to stop and become aware of this tendency trying to surface. Instead, I began to exercise the good that is me, as opposed to being sucked in by everything bad, which is easy!

I've chosen to exercise the power of not reacting, but rather be proactive to eliminate negative behavior. Bad choices often make good stories, but this one is meant to expand your consciousness towards growth and awareness. I feel good about my ability to use adversity to learn and teach, knowing that I was once severely wounded myself. Tough times don't last, unless you choose to allow them to linger.

So I remain in the process of releasing and letting go of any pent-up emotions of anger, disappointment or resentment. Instead, I stake claim to being guided by love, and it's impossible to think of a genuine revolutionary lacking this quality. My hero Minister Malcolm was certainly driven by his love of Black and oppressed people. Anger, insecurity, selfishness and impatience no longer hinder my vision; it remains open and clear.

Keep in mind that we're all going through something, and you never know what someone might be struggling with. Therefore, I try to keep myself filled with gratitude along with the awareness of being an example of peace and serenity.

The road to recovery is a never-ending journey, and Black people can never take for granted our deep-rooted issues surrounding our mental health. Many suffer from post-traumatic syndrome stemming from the horrors of slavery: family separated, women brutally raped, men stripped of their dignity. These conditions grew greater after the signing of the Emancipation Proclamation. Our people may have been freed physically from the chains on our bodies, but the horror of reconstruction, inequality and racial disparities remain, such as is illustrated in innumerable unjust police killings.

All of this has kept our minds mentally chained, and many continue wearing the mask to cover our emotional suffering, which has been turned inwards and leads to self-destructive behavior. Psychiatrist Dr. Francis Cress Welsing, who came into prominence in the 1970s with her book entitled, *The Isis Papers: The Keys to the Colors,* contends that racism is a fear of genetic annihilation that causes the desire to control and destroy people of color.

Melanin is the pigment that gives skin its color, and darker-skinned people have more melanin in their skin than people who are classified as White. So when dark mates with light and a baby of color is produced, we can reflect on her theory of fear of White genetic annihilation. Whether you agree or disagree with her theory, it helps in eliminating the emotions when considering racism. The systematic oppression of Black Americans is deeply embedded in the fabric of American culture—a nation made up of immigrants.

But Blacks are the only people who were forcibly brought here and kept as slaves for hundreds of years. Although racism afflicts many ethnic groups, it's been justified by a racist ideology derived from slavery and the apartheid system of Jim Crow that insisted on Black inferiority to Whites. The remnants of this evil and ugly past still emerge, and it doesn't help when you have mass media promoting fear and stereotypical views.

Crime is usually committed against those who are closest, but you'll never hear much about White on White crime projected in media. Why? Because society wants to lift those who are White and allow that which is Black to destroy itself. This is why there are liquor stores and churches on every corner in the Black community—to keep us drunk and intoxicated by religion. Why is it that you're so easily able to find guns, drugs and other vices, things which aren't even manufactured in our neighborhoods?

Mass incarceration has become big business, employing thousands of professionals with the vested interest of maintaining large, privately-owned prison populations that continue to be filled by people of color. The underlying message is that Black life isn't significant—but the change lies in our hands.

The late, great Reverend Dr. Martin L. King Jr. once stated that love can transform enemies into friends. I can agree, based on my own dilemma in dealing with anger, that anger will not create a peaceful planet. I seek to contribute towards doing my part to manifest a world of peace by drastically changing me and the way I think.

Upon becoming a Marine, my former boxing trainer, the late Mr. Tom Browner, kind of got inside my head and rattled me a bit. He'd said that the Marines would be good in making me meaner, which generated negative dialogue inside my head of being mean and nasty. I know many who'd say, "You don't have to try, you already are," but back then, my coach verbalizing this made me uncomfortable.

Looking back through more mature lenses, I'm quite proud of the work that I continue to do in manifesting a better me and breaking down the walls that once confined my greatness. My temper still exists, but I've learned to better deal with my frustrations. I have come to respect our unique and differing personalities as human beings, not Black or White, but human.

Depression is a big culprit in our community, and it played a major role in me not being a consistent fighter. I recall a respected trainer of the U.S. Navy, who trained some of the fighters I competed against. He said, "Son, I just don't understand. You have so much natural talent. In one fight, you look like a future champ ready to make his mark, and then in others, you look as if you really don't care."

The truth of the matter was when depression sank in, I didn't care. I had no real awareness of this back then, but I do remember getting caught with the right punch that would put me down for the final count. I experienced those feelings of wanting to die in the ring, as if this would be a courageous and honorable way for me to die. What was tough came in knowing plenty of fighters who were able to turn their rage into success, but we're all different and on different paths.

A friend comes to mind. We knew each other during our years of boxing and even sparred against each other a few times. He was enshrined into the D.C. Boxing Hall of Fame, but we met in the year 1987, shortly after I returned home after a tour of duty in Japan. Tony 'Da Beast' Suggs was known locally and nationally, knocking out nearly every one of his opponents. His story is very similar to my own of overcoming adversity, and I am so grateful for our current friendship. Today we continue to support each other in the fight called life.

Tony was one fight away from representing our country in the 1988 Olympics, but he was knocked down by tragedy when he was flown home to mourn the death of his infant daughter Ashley, who died of SIDS. This sent his life on a tailspin; his drug addiction escalated, and he found himself in and out of prison, feeling mad at God for allowing his baby girl to die. By way of a renewed faith, my brother is using his story to help others, and this is our purpose.

For me, my blessings didn't translate into me reaching such success as a fighter, but my story, like his, is a source of inspiration in overcoming challenging life experiences. Today, I am filled with gratitude in no longer feeling the weight of the world on my shoulders. I've made drastic changes in my life that have increased my mental, physical and spiritual well-being, allowing me to speak loud and clear that I am a Revolutionary. My change is all about love and my evolution as a man who seeks to inspire others.

CHAPTER 5

PEACE BEGINS WITH ME

Rather than waiting for conditions to shift around me, I allow peace to express itself within. I take a deep, focused breath, pause, and affirm inside my head. Peace begins with me. Then I slowly release, letting go of any and all negativity, repeating and confirming that peace begins with me. I shift into a vessel of infinite peace, my mere presence enables me to influence others by being an example of peace and harmony that ultimately spreads to influence the world.

Angry people cannot create a peaceful planet.

The above affirmation is on display in my work area, serving the purpose of helping me maintain calm or focus. We're all forced to find constructive ways to manage and deal with the various personalities of people, who themselves just might be doing the same in trying to deal with you, here in a world surrounded by chaos and dysfunction.

It's said with age comes wisdom and maturity. Over the years, I've become more aware of the significance of simply being still. I've learned that I don't necessarily have to express my opinion or respond to nonsense; often, it's best to keep my opinion to myself.

We live in a rapidly changing world. The mind is constantly bombarded with mental chatter that has the potential to negatively ignite our emotions and make us feel like we're standing on shaky ground. The only way to counteract chaos is with stillness, by breathing deeply, generating calm and focusing—diving into the quieter waters to slow down, plan, refocus or reflect.

Every day, we have plenty of opportunities to get angry, stressed or offended, but when we allow these negative emotions to take over, we've allowed something or someone to get inside our head and steal joy. However, mastering inner peace helps us hear when God speaks. It helps us stay engaged in conversation with God throughout the day, continually giving thanks and following the path of calm.

I've learned that inner peace can only be reached when we practice forgiveness.

Dr. Martin L. King Jr. once stated that darkness cannot drive out darkness; only light can do that. So we must develop and maintain the capacity to forgive and be that light.

These few words are so simple, yet contain a message so profound. Few realize that the enemy many of us have is ourselves—living in constant fear and worry. This is the absolute opposite of the nature of our own divine essence, to experience love and peace.

I learned this lesson firsthand in forgiving my father who raised me and accepting him for who he was. He didn't always show love, at least not to me, but we all see and respond to things differently. I'll only speculate from the point of view of being raised by a man who often made me feel that his frustrations were taken out on me.

In understanding the male ego like I do, it's my belief that his ego played a role in the abuse of a boy who closely resembled his biological father, especially after drinking. I was that Black boy over there, running scared. And my ole man who raised me had a problem. He'd get deep inside the bottle, and I'd become his physical and verbal punching bag.

I can now consider my biological father's perspective. I was conceived by his infidelity, and he stayed clear, especially after my mother married two years later. In that same year, my mother gave birth to her second son. I recall being told by my mother as a young adult how her new husband accepted me as being his son and verbally gave me his name. But then things began to change after the birth of my brother, and I became Darrick, caught in the middle.

I heard whispers amongst family on my mother's side: "It don't make sense the way he treat Darrick. He ain't even that boy's father."

Eventually, my curiosity arose, and when the truth was revealed, I mumbled under my breath, "Good, I can't stand the mother fucker."

I now know my reaction was simply my feelings being hurt due to rejection. This certainly affected my inner peace.

Over the years, I am better able to control the rage that dwells inside me. I have learned to listen more and speak less, and in doing so, I've become more compassionate. I can take into consideration that someone's sensitivity could be related to my own. We can never fully know what someone might be going through, and we must recognize the power of listening—which has the potential to generate harmony and respect.

Slowing down and being still has helped me find joy in listening to my own thoughts, some of which are God speaking his guidance. I've learned to allow people to be who they are without being overly critical, though sometimes this is easier said than actually done. My lifetime of experiences has taught me how to adjust to the differences in people.

As mentioned, we all wear various masks, such as the mask of social acceptance, that may vary depending on the company you're in. Every situation is different, and playing this game called life is much easier if we are in a peaceful state. It takes practice to be patient and courteous while taking the time to listen to the concerns of others. We don't have to always add our two cents; often, people just want to get the situation off their chest.

I've learned how to adjust to various people and occasions in the age of sensationalism, which sells regardless of whether it's true. I try to rid myself of being overly critical of others, especially in the age of social media, where words are often misinterpreted based on how one may feel about another person, be it good or bad.

I feel uncomfortable dominating a conversation, no matter how well versed I may be in it, so I try to leave space in between my words and allow others in. I understand the value of listening, which serves to assist in becoming a better leader.

"A wise old owl lived in an oak, the more he saw, the less he spoke. The less he spoke, the more he heard. Why can't we all be like that wise old bird?"

During the early stages of life, we're all taught to speak. This is an important milestone in a child's development; however, listening is an equally, if not a more, important skill that is often overlooked by parents and educators alike. We were all taught (hopefully) to listen to our parents and teachers. However, few of us were taught about the significance of good listening—the active, disciplined kind of listening that helps us examine and challenge the information we hear.

Good listening is the key to developing fresh insights and ideas that fuel success. Now that I've become more aware of its significance, I often challenge myself to become a better student of listening. In doing so, I've discovered how many people listen just enough to respond rather than truly opening so to understand another's concerns. It takes discipline to put our own thoughts and ideas on hold to support another—and in the process, become a better person.

I recall not so long ago when I facilitated a Men's empowerment group known as The Gathering of Men. I often had to remind cats of my generation to listen and allow the young people to speak, because we tend to constantly be talking about how we did things back in the day. That day is long gone, though, and our young people have different challenges. We can also learn from them by simply listening, and as I continue to grow in faith, I've discovered that it's not about finding yourself as opposed to continually re-creating yourself. This has made my life much more interesting, and God is indeed the director of my journey.

I'm proud to be an advocate of uplifting energy, and believe that conflict and drama cannot continue without my participation; we have a choice in whatever arises during the course of our lives.

CHAPTER 6

INFORMATION IS POWER

The early 1960s was a time of revolution—a drastic change in our society was needed.

I was quite young in the 1960s, but I paid attention to things pertaining to Black people and our struggle. I began to read about things that came to light during that time.

The 60s was a time when Black folk had grown sick and tired of being pushed around and treated like second-class citizens. Some, such as activist, playwright and poet Amari Baraka (formerly known as Leroi Jones), viewed the 1960s as America's third revolution, the Negro revolution that was meant to change the socially unjust, racist climate in which we still live.

Racism may not be as blatant as it once was, but it's still rampant. In my opinion, the 2016 election of Donald J Trump as president is a good indication that race in America is still a major factor that must be dealt with, and drastic change is still very much needed.

I recall how my young mind was heavily influenced by the rise of Black pride in the 1970s—where many friends claim I remain. But the

80s is when I started reading about people and movements happening around me. I read about Minister Malcolm X being tragically killed in 1965 and how his influence brought forth the emergence of the Black Panther party. They tried to combat police brutality as well as serve as a vanguard of the Black community, with breakfast and health programs for those in need. Sadly, their efforts were resisted by our U.S. government as different chapters of the BP party sprung up in cities throughout America. I read of how in April of 1967, heavyweight boxing champion Muhammad Ali refused to join the Army and fight for a country that had demonstrated an unwillingness to fight for Black Americans. I read of the tragic assassination of a King—the Reverend Dr. Martin L. King, Jr.—on April 4, 1968, twenty-three days before my sixth birthday.

I have a memory of leaving Washington, D.C., which was burning along with many other cities throughout the nation in defiance of the tragic assassination of Dr. King. Six months later, I recall the medal ceremony in the Olympics on October 16, 1968, in Mexico City that saw John Carlos and Tommy Smith raise their Black-gloved fists during the playing of the anthem. Carlos, Smith and Australian silver medalist Peter Norman also all wore human rights badges on their jacket.

I'd learn many years later while listening to an interview with both Smith and Carlos that the gesture was not a Black Power salute, as was touted by the media, but rather a sign of empowering the human rights of oppressed people around the world. This same idea was advocated by Malcolm X before he was gunned down.

These are just a few of the events that my young mind began to absorb, which fueled my Black pride and consciousness to higher levels. My attention was captured by news clips of revolutionary actions taking place in our rapidly changing society. I recall seeing flag-draped coffins returning home from Vietnam. I remember the Black soldiers in particular, many of whom were physically or emotionally crippled, returning home to a country they'd sacrificed their lives for and where they were still treated like second-class citizens.

In 2016, mainstream Americans increasingly became unsettled by Black NFL players kneeling and executing an honorable gesture in their attempt to bring awareness to the sad epidemic and long history of unarmed Black men being killed by law enforcement.

I strongly support Colin Kaepernick and the movement that has since ended with Kaepernick being unofficially banned from playing in the NFL. I'm sure that many aren't even aware of the original version of the National Anthem, which references the killing of our ancestors (slaves).

No refuge could save the hireling and slave

from the terror of flight or the gloom of the grave.

And the star-spangled banner in triumph doth wave

o'er the land of the free and the home of the brave.

Today, the world continues to see countless numbers of unarmed Black people being killed by police. In the age of cell phone video, we now see so much of what we were not supposed to: A black man being shot multiple times in the back, hands up, a gesturing of surrender.

Black Lives Matter is nothing new; it's reminiscent of yesteryear during the Civil Rights movement. We must remain aware that hate is perpetuated by people in power who feel a sense of privilege.

CHAPTER 7

PEACE AND CLOSURE

My words are meant to convince that you, too, can overcome adversity by facing those challenging times that life sometimes presents, knowing that they are nothing more than teachable moments. Change lies in learning from disappointment, and adversity is a teacher!

One day I simply stopped, looked fear in the eye and refused to back down in recognizing the value of me. I broke free of the shackles that once kept me mentally incarcerated, and being the fighter I am, I've gained added strength to escape self-imposed limitations.

I have used the written and spoken word as therapy, reaping the benefits of looking back at my journey. I am grateful to now be able to articulate my anger without being overwhelmed with guilt or doubt. I remember the confused boy who often cried inside the man, but through faith and belief in myself, I can stay in control of my actions.

We face two sides before committing to action. On one side is our emotions: a physical response to change that which is hard-wired and universal. The other side is our feelings: mental associations and reactions to things that are personal and acquired through negative experiences.

So, in other words, emotions precede feelings. I recall many moments of feeling unwelcomed amongst so-called family, often drifting off unnoticed and feeling a little jealous of the favored kids. Through study, I learned that a child that feels neglected can often develop a very independent outlook on life. That feeling of solitude can be tough on a child's mental and emotional well-being.

When children feel safe, they ask questions, learn to trust, share feelings and grow. I was often afraid, even when I knew the answer. I was still afraid it would be the wrong answer, or that I would ask too many questions.

I recall not long after both my brother and I had gotten out of the Marines. It was one of the first times I really opened up about my rage and anger towards our father: his biological dad and the same father that treated me like crap and made clear I was no Chapman. I laid everything out—how uncomfortable it still was to be in his presence, about having nightmares of physically harming him and his brother.

He listened, and tears were shed. But not long after, my brother calls and asks if I want to go to the racetrack. I agree, and he picks me up. I'm in good spirits, when suddenly I notice that he's turning up the street leading to our father's house. I felt so disrespected, like my feelings I'd shared earlier were neglected.

I angrily replied, "Damn, don't you have enough consideration after all that was said to at least ask me if I minded being in his presence?"

I sat in the back seat and didn't say a word, but felt as if I wanted to let loose a barrage of rage. When we get to the track, I was faced with my other nightmare: my father's brother and other men, who only added to my feelings of discomfort and betrayal. I was able to manage my anger, but right then and there, my heart closed. I was determined not to allow anyone else in for quite some time.

Later that year, my brother remarried and relocated on the west coast as I continued in my efforts to peel back layers of a painful past. I had since separated from the mother of my children and was fully invested in the community, steadily improving as a motivational speaker and poet. Still, I rarely shared with my family the things that I was proudly participating in. On this particular occasion, I had been invited to spit poetry and speak at some type of outdoor celebration in Washington, D.C. My brother just happened to be in town, and I told him I would be speaking.

I was surprised that he came. Sharing my poetry was easier, but in speaking, I often went within. I recall the discomfort in knowing that my brother was in the audience. I'm sure I'd told him about the things I was doing, but still, I was nervous and feeling vulnerable.

At the end of my performance, I embraced the applause of the audience and looked into the eyes of my brother. He warmly embraced me and said, "Bra, that was powerful, and I understand you much better."

I guess you can say that I've always been an actor in the way I was able to hide the darkness felt within me. So, in turn, my soul became hardened. I'd feel the effects of a world that teaches a boy that a man doesn't cry or show his emotions, although the boy inside of me cried quite often. As I looked back through the mirror of my soul, I recognized the depth of my educational challenges and how being labeled stupid made me fearful of asking questions.

I dug deeper into reading, trying to better understand mental health issues with the goal of better understanding me. I began to question whether I had a learning disability due to such factors as—

- Difficulty in remembering
- Problems with math skills
- Trouble paying attention
- Trouble following directions
- Poor coordination
- Problems staying organized

With strong determination, I've gotten much better in these areas and ultimately made it through high school. I've never been diagnosed as having a learning disability, but I continue to push forward and find value in educating myself through reading, so to move beyond the miseducation that we all receive in America.

I am proud of my brilliance, and the fighter in me will continue to push forward, knocking out whatever opposition life may present. I've always been a sensitive kid, who is now a sensitive man. I've tried ignoring my feelings by hiding the emotional hurt and pain that came my way. I felt uncomfortable confiding in anyone, and this tension would eventually erupt like a volcano upon individuals that on many occasions didn't deserve my angry words and actions. I still wear my emotions on my sleeve and have to remind myself not to take things so personally. I've gotten much better, though—we're all works in progress.

When I was around twelve, I started smoking weed to escape my reality, a habit that would greatly increase as I grew in years. I was also a heavy drinker, and preferred to alienate myself from family and friends. The effects of being high only heightened my sensitivities, and I would get kicked out of school for fighting—mainly due to me being unable to control my emotions.

My mother once confided in her mother about her troubled son. I'll never forget her saying sarcastically, "Boy, mamma seems to think you suicidal and want to kill yourself."

My tough outer demeanor raised up in a defensive posture to shield my pride in admitting my grandmother being on point. I laughed it off, but deep down, I was hurt by my mother's reaction, which showed a lack of concern about my well-being.

I went through many highs and lows not long after graduating high school, which is when depression really hit. I remember thinking, "She is going to feel bad when I follow through and do it." I used to jog up and down the highway doing my boxing roadwork in the wee hours of the morning, tears streaming down my face. I recall an occasion or two contemplating veering out into oncoming morning rush traffic to put an end to my suffering.

My youth was spent always fighting, and around age sixteen, I quit all other sports and started to compete only in boxing. This helped me to gain discipline and better channel my anger, although no one took the time to come to my fights and cheer me on or support my efforts. My parents just showed no interest. I somewhat understood Mom; she was against me boxing from the start, being afraid I might get hurt.

Pops showed no interest whatsoever either. But he was quick to brag to his friends when intoxicated about how once he and a buddy came downstairs to see me working out on the heavy bag. Knowing they were watching, I'd picked up the speed and intensity. As my pop started to brag about how good a boxer I was, for a brief moment, I felt happy being shown attention. But it soon faded in knowing that, except for that moment, he had never taken the time to even come into our basement.

A White neighbor took me to my first fight. He'd learned of me through his son, Tommy, who was cool with my brother and me. Tommy, my brother and I loaded up in his van, and he took me out to Maryland for my very first boxing match. Deep down, it bothered me that my parents—especially my dad after bragging to his friend—showed no interest.

I completed my military service at twenty-seven. That was pretty late in the game to become a professional boxer, and I hadn't given it any real thought in turning pro. But boxing brought me joy, so I took a physical, signed the necessary documents, and received a professional boxer's license. After hearing the buzz of me being a good fighter, my pops finally came. He was impressed, and I was proud to see him become a fan. He supported the remainder of my in and out, up and down boxing career.

It's an amazing feeling to be able to articulate things that happened many years ago. Studies show that when people write about emotionally charged episodes, they experience marked improvement in their mental, emotional and physical well-being. In my own research, I've been able to smile more and stress a lot less. I continue to remain mindful of my actions and reflecting a positive light. I'm honored to serve as a model of how writing has helped me become a much better person, who has found peace and closure in increasing my faith, building trust, letting go and allowing God!

THE GATHERING OF MEN and guests enjoyed a great discussion of *"Is a man or woman perfect or complete without the other?"*

CHAPTER 8

THE POWER OF FORGIVENESS

Forgiveness is essential for growth and happiness; holding onto the past harms us far more than the offender. Forgiveness frees us to live in the present moment, but when we keep reliving the wrong that was done, we remain in the past—which causes us to miss the beauty of today. We've all experienced situations that have taken us time to recover from. And as we move through them, we must remain open and aware that times often are not as bad as we think. We just need more time to recover, and recovery starts with a willingness to forgive.

We must not allow whatever predicament we find ourselves in to define us.

When things are put in proper perspective—when we're able to move beyond what happened and who did what—we can now learn something from it. Life's unfavorable moments have a way of teaching us, and I am grateful to have learned many lessons from the various challenges that I've faced throughout my life journey. Forgiveness doesn't mean that you forget the past; instead, you look upon it with a greater sense of compassion.

This memoir is dedicated to my fathers: John Bug Marshal, my biological dad who I never fully got a chance to know as well as I would have liked, and George Walter Chapman, the man who raised me. These men were the inspiration behind this creative work, though it's hardly due to me seeing them as good role models. But in their own rough and rugged ways, they were good men. I can honestly say that despite the negativity that has been transferred to me, the son of them both, I pay homage to their spirits as I continue in my efforts to be a good model of manhood and inspire the next generation to better understand our significance as men.

I surely don't want to add to the many riches that already exist inside the grave when God calls me home to enter the gates of heaven—a reference from the book *Understanding Your Potential* by the late Dr. Myles Monroe. I continue to learn from his many books, online lectures and writings, and he has definitely left behind a legacy—which is something we should all seek to do. I was introduced to Mr. Monroe by my first cousin, Bishop Jason L. Johnson, who is just as strong-willed and stubborn as me. He made his drastic change from who he was to the beauty of who he is now—a man saving souls in the Christian ministry—back when we were in our 20s.

Dr. Monroe states that everything in life was created with potential. In every seed there is a tree, in every bird there is a flock, in every fish there is a school, and in every boy and girl, there is a man and woman bursting with potential. The problem is that our potential is often buried in the grave with us, and in turn, the cemetery becomes one of the richest places on Earth. The Bible tells many stories about the abilities our creator has planted within us. We were all sent to the world with a limitless amount of potential, but few draw their full extent. It's a tragedy that with over seven billion people on this planet today, only a small percentage will experience the abundance of their gifts and talents.

I refuse to be a contributor to the wealth that already exists inside cemeteries around the world. Our potential was not given to be deposited in the grave when we physically leave the world. There are many selves within that lie dormant, untapped and unused. God is always seeking to pull out what may not yet be visible, for he created more than what's evident on the outside. The tragedy lies in the minute we begin to settle and be satisfied with where we are in our lives, when we lose the possibility of revealing what lies inside of us.

My life continues to demonstrate my toughness as I travel through the rough and rugged terrain of the valley. In the words of my all-time favorite artist, Mr. Curtis Mayfield, "I'm a winner, and I won't allow anyone to say, I can't make it, because a feeble mind is in my way…" One that will never convince me that I can't make it.

I remember the truth being revealed about my biological father when I was around fifteen. He stood me up the first time we were supposed to officially meet. I knew who he was, though, and had seen him around. I recall occasionally hearing whispers through the grapevine of adult conversation about who was and wasn't my father. When he was angry or disappointed in me, my father who raised me would say I sure wasn't one of them. I was finally made aware that he and his brother James were actually speaking truth to me.

This feeling of being an outsider molded me and became the foundation of my rough and tough exterior. That revelation is not meant to blame, but rather encourage others to recognize the significance of speaking your truth so to empower YOU.

My own truth came a few years after deciding to be known by my name given at birth, despite haven gone through school and serving my country under Chapman. I had two identities. I was known as Darrick Chapman, but legally Darrick Johnson was on my birth record, driver's license and social security card. It wasn't until I got out of the military that this became a real problem. Basically, I had two identities. So, I said to myself, why go through the headache of legally changing my last name to one that I never felt a sense of connection to? I decided in 1990 to be known by my birth name of Johnson, and it was very traumatic.

After I got married in 1992, people had no idea how on edge I was. I recall being ridiculed after getting married by some guys: "I thought the woman is supposed to change her last name by taking on the name of her husband, not the other way around!"

"F-you, punk. Johnson is my last name as well as my wife's."

The years that followed were very mentally and emotionally challenging. I even went through some of this within my family, despite them knowing the truth all along. But in my auntie's defense, I had lived under the name of Chapman for some twenty-something years prior. So when she announced me at some family function as Darrick Chapman, I quickly corrected her. Still, I was bothered by her "whatever" response.

After my mother revealed the truth concerning my father and me, I immediately began to reflect upon all the verbal and physical abuse I'd endured. But I've learned over the years how a young man craves a sense of validation from the father figure in his life. So I interpret my response now as me being more hurt than angry, due to my feeling that I was unworthy of being his son.

Still, both of these men—my biological father and the man who raised me—are very much a part of the man I've come to be. In their own separate ways, they molded the tough outer shell that surrounds my true loving nature. One that I unconsciously feared being revealed, whereas today, I am grateful that fear no longer exists in my life. I now realize had my unconscious fear been left unchecked, my forward progress would have been altered. Maybe I'd be dead or in jail, still trying to find a sense of joy and peace in my life.

So discovering the will and recognizing the power of forgiveness is the most important spiritual principle I have learned in the course of my journey. I learned that forgiveness doesn't let you forget the wrongs, but it allows you to release and let go of all the hurt holding you back. Forgiveness serves as a prerequisite for finding personal peace and discovering your gifts.

My biological father and I had a very strong resemblance to one another, especially when he was younger. But never did we establish a real relationship, despite being in his presence on several occasions. At his big birthday parties, we'd acknowledge each other and then go our separate ways, mingling and drinking. I remember at one of them, I had been drinking heavily because I didn't want to go home and deal with the drama between me and the mother of my children.

Leaving after midnight, I would have made it safely had I gone home, because I was not far away. But I turned into the city and made an illegal U-turn. I was pulled over, arrested and charged with a DUI, then released in the wee hours of the morning. Feeling like crap, I walked from the police station to the waterfront where my car was parked in the lot of the fish market. When I reached it, I didn't get into my car at first. Instead, I stood there, staring into the Potomac River, feeling so bad that I felt the urge to jump in and end my life.

This was one of the moments that I thank God that I became a coward—or rather wise—enough to not be directed by my emotions. I got in my car, tears streaming down my face, and headed home. I abandoned drinking for the next few years, though when I felt myself falling in love again, it brought me back to the bottle.

I'm being humorous, but now I am more responsible when I drink, especially when behind the wheel.

I'm grateful to be able to physically share this as opposed to you reading these words after my death. I recall visiting my biological father a week or so before he died. We sat in his living room, and I recognized familiar traits like his emotionless, straight-to-the-point demeanor and mannerisms. Everything said between us was one- and two-word answers, due to us really not knowing each other. Even when he was healthy, we never had much to say, and I got the sense I was looking at myself years down the road.

I also recall feeling that my anger wasn't directed towards him in the same manner as my father who raised me. I came from his seed, but I didn't know Bug Marshal. So I was able to function in his absence.

I once attended a ceremony honoring my biological dad as the Father of the Year in his Indian Head community. I don't quite remember, but I'm almost certain that my mother, in her manipulating way, convinced me to go. I recall sitting there, speechless, actually wondering why I was even there, as his other siblings spoke his praises.

Then, after he transitioned in 2011, I recall my father who raised me acknowledging John Marshal for the first time as being my dad in expressing his condolences to me the day before he was to be buried.

Two years later, George Chapman who raised me also transitioned. I recall the pastor who was supposed to conduct the viewing services being a no-show, so my brother Jeff, who was in the early stages of the ministry, took the lead in eulogizing his father. My sister Crystal and I assisted him in honoring our father, and afterwards we received praise from his older brother Jackie for our efforts.

But I recall the difficulty of speaking my truth due to the fear of it being misinterpreted. I spoke of how different my relationship with our father was in comparison to that which he shared with Jeff and Crystal. I did so diplomatically, and concluded with understanding the need to forgive. He and I had been having a good relationship in his final years. Still, I was somewhat rattled when a co-worker said how George always talked about his kids, looking dead at me as if he were saying to himself, "Did George ever make mention of a second son?"

There was a part of me who anticipated him saying, "Oh yeah, you must be the boxer. He did make mention of a son who boxed." But that never came.

I just remember taking a deep breath and refusing to allow this to bother me. But deep down, it did. Others would come up and share their remembrances, and I wondered if anyone other than me picked up that I was not acknowledged as one of George's children, despite sitting there beside my brother and sister and mother in the first pew. From there, my mind raced, even going back to high school. My father's sisters were both guidance counselors, yet they never tried to counsel me, the frightened kid who was being physically and emotionally battered by their brothers.

I've learned to turn to God as opposed to man as I forgive myself. It's my belief that we're all battling through something, and only God knows anything about it. It's important to be careful with our words, as they can only be forgiven but not forgotten, and again I take a deep breath and give thanks for the therapeutic expression of my thoughts. I feel very confident that both my earthly fathers smile down with a sense of pride from the heavens above as their spirits bear witness to me, their son, carrying on the strong legacy of them both!

The poem below was originally written somewhere around 2003-

4, not long after my introduction to theatre. At the time when I wrote this poem and expressed it with so much passion at the historic Lincoln Theatre in Washington, D.C., I had no idea about the complexities in forgiving or the courage it took being vulnerable, spitting this piece before my father who raised me and whom it was generated towards. This became the beginning of me doing the needed work towards my salvation, which in turn changed the dynamics of the very strained relationship between my father and me. It wasn't until after this performance that I felt in my heart I had actually forgiven them both, and our relationships would drastically change towards being better.

Nerves jumping, taking deep breaths, I'm trying to relax and maintain composure just before what was to be my biggest performance to date. Suddenly, I hear my name: "Darrick Johnson, aka Brother Malcolm, now coming to the stage." I am filled with excitement and a tad bit of worry of the poem being locked in memory, hoping my mind wouldn't suddenly draw a blank. I graced the stage with confidence, then quickly noticed a look of intensity glaring directly at me as I appeared before the audience. It was almost as if the audience had faded off into the distance as the boy inside the man suddenly felt an all-too-familiar intimidation.

I grabbed the little boy by the hand and took over.

FORGIVENESS

Forgiveness means that you're willing to release and let go, so to make room for CHANGE

Standing tall and firm, ready to challenge yourself to move according to your own domain,

Which does not mean that you forget whatever happened, but non-forgiveness keeps you stuck

Filled with anger and resentment…

So take charge of your life with a willingness to forgive, by allowing unresolved issues to fade off into the distance, because not letting go will ultimately drive you insane.

Grateful am I to have forgiven. In turn, my life has been much better, and I'm able to enjoy more of what life has to offer...

Like, for instance, finding true love that my anger seemed to sometimes hinder...

This journey of redemption began by first forgiving myself for the many times I wondered

Why I couldn't be like everyone else, as if they were the standards, as if something were wrong with me...

No longer do I fear admitting former insecurities. Currently, I am feeling good, appreciative and proud of my beauty—

I also forgave parents who were obviously unaware of how their past

Unresolved hurts and pains could move on to negatively strain generations after generation

if one doesn't decide to break the chain of pain with forgiveness.

So are you ready and willing to be the one who brings forth CHANGE in eventually putting a halt

To unnecessary, lingering pain that will continue without a willingness to break the mental and emotional chains of dysfunction that is ever so present in our community.

So we must recognize that forgiveness is the key that allows our brain to open up, breaking new ground towards a higher level of consciousness, starting an evolutionary process going straight to the heart.

FORGIVENESS is where it all starts as you experience inner peace and love of God

to the fullest

And it all starts with forgiveness...

My father came backstage and gave me a big, warm hug. He is a man of few words, but said, "I'm proud of you boy. You ah damn good speaker."

And in this moment, I knew. I had finally forgiven.

R.I.P. John Bug Marshal, who made me and George Walter Chapman, who raised me.

CHAPTER 9

SAYING GOODBYE TO YESTERDAY IS HARD

There has been lots of soul searching during this project, and in the process of doing so, God called home some of my childhood friends. They grew up with me in a predominantly White neighborhood that our families integrated in the early 1970s in Waldorf, Maryland, and each of them in their own way played a significant role in shaping the man I am.

Steve Cornish was a year or so older than me. While most say that I'm ole school to the core, well, Steve was one of those cats that turned me on to many of those back in the day groups from the latter part of the funk era that I still enjoy listening to today, groups like Cameo, Lakeside and the Bar-Kays. Steve had all the albums growing up (whereas today I have the CDs), and we'd sit in his room, smoking weed while getting hyped talking about the graphics on his various albums.

William Pierre Strong… Slick Pierre moved into our neighborhood somewhere between 1978-80 from Palmer Park, Maryland, which is famously known as being the home of all-time boxing great, Sugar Ray

Leonard. Early on in getting to know him, I saw him as trying to take my shine as the ladies' man of the neighborhood and the brother with the sharpest hands. Our stories are very similar in the sense that neither one of us lived up to our athletic potential. Pierre was a track star, or rather, could have been, like me. We tried living two lives as athletes who liked to party all the time, smoking weed, often quenching thirst with an ole English 800. Nine times out of ten, it just doesn't work because the two don't mix.

My funniest memory of him was after school one day. Pierre was looking sharp in slacks and a nice pair of shoes. We're lounging, then we see this guy who was the star receiver of the varsity football team back in the day. Pierre was smooth and slick; he never got loud when talking shit, and he started to get inside the head of the so-called speedy receiver. Pierre is boasting, and we're backing the challenge he'll beat my man in the 50-yard dash. The dude accepts, and Pierre smokes him in slacks and dress shoes.

Then there's Vance Boyd, at least three or more years my junior and my unofficial younger brother. He moved to the neighborhood around 1977 and was my other fat friend that I started out teasing. I recall a night around 1980. Chuck was the only one in our crew who had his own car at the time, although my brother and I would often steal our parents' car to take the crew joyriding. On this night, I believe it was me, Chuck, Vance and maybe Maurice loaded in Chuck's Pinto. We'd ride deep, and five dollars would nearly push the gas gauge beyond half a tank, so you had to have at least two in the tank, and the rest went for weed and brew—which speaks to how we could stretch a dollar during the time. We went downtown to a hot spot back then on New York Avenue called The Room. DJ Kool wasn't well known back then outside of D.C., and I think you needed to be at least sixteen to get in. Vance was like fourteen, so I gave him a pair of my glasses frames. (Back then, it was in style to wear glasses with no lenses; we wanted to look distinguished, but still hard.)

So Vance got into the club and we had a ball. When we came out, it was early morning and none of us knew the city that well. Eventually, we made it back to Waldorf. I crept into the house and crawled into bed, and I'm certain mamma dragged me up and out of bed to go to church a few hours later.

Big Benny transitioned before Steve, Pierre and Vance. He was my main man, and we faced similar challenges, which made us connect, although we never talked about them. He was one of the first brothers I'd met when moving to this lily-white community somewhere around 1974. Our friendship bonded when we were middle schoolers after he got fed up with me teasing him about being fat. On this hot, sunny day, he had a large patch of moisture under his armpits. I went in, clowning like I thought I was Richard Pryor.

"Man, your armpits so moist looks as if someone took a cup of water and threw it under them. Flies can't stand the funk."

Everyone is laughing, and it's always been my nature to take things a little too far. I start flicking jabs in his face, and he started glaring like a dog, preparing to attack. This actually egged me on, and I got a little too relaxed while pushing the envelope.

Suddenly, Benny grabbed me by the collar and commenced to toss my lightweight self across the lunch table like a human missile. The cafeteria erupted in laughter, followed by the anticipation of a fight! Administrators quickly came and broke us up, respect was gained, and our bond was built.

His older brother Milton, who I also became friends with, once told me that Benny said in speaking about me, "That lil' skinny runt got heart."

Benny was a big inspiration in me pursuing boxing, which we enjoyed watching on TV. The 1970s was the greatest era in Heavyweight boxing history, and Benny would often come over on Friday night and watch fights with me and my dad. I recall him having a life-size poster of Muhammad Ali in his bedroom, while my favorite during this time was Ken Norton. He'd started out as a relatively unknown fighter who just so happened to be a former U.S. Marine, and he was my inspiration to become an All-Marine boxer.

I'll never forget the Christmas he got a pair of boxing gloves, and my house immediately became our neighborhood Madison Square Garden. On warm days, we'd be on the patio, which was the size of a boxing ring, or in the basement where we'd move the furniture and the ring was a big square rug. All the guys in the neighborhood would come around, especially during the summer, and we'd have daily bouts. The main event was usually me and big Benny, who outweighed me by at least a hundred pounds, or a match between me and my nemesis cousin, Jason, who was so damn fast and always trying to break me down in front of my crew. Yes, I'd get mad, but when it got too intense, he'd back off and we'd go back to being brothers.

Word quickly spread of boxing in our neighborhood, and the Dirk (which was how the Dog Patch Boys pronounced my name) was pretty good with the hands. This made me a target, especially to those who knew me as the skinny shy kid who used to live there. Most young men of my generation possessed a natural competitive spirit, and we'd challenge each other—especially when it came to toughness. It was a part of growing up, and if you stood your ground, respect was usually earned.

Benny and I were quite a duo, and when we weren't boxing or actually fighting in defense of our dignity, our days were spent riding around the neighborhood on our dirt bikes, drinking, smoking weed and even a little horseback riding. Butch, Benny's father, owned a horse. It was walking distance to the stable, and we'd occasionally go there and ride.

These experiences and so many others were the beginning of a short-lived but powerful bond between us, and we both escaped the mental and physical traumas of our broken homes in the form of drugs and alcohol. This meant we were easily provoked into fighting our White peers, who enjoyed calling us Niggers when they had us outnumbered. Benny and I hardly ever backed down from such odds, but we also knew when to haul ass and get the hell out of Dodge. We were crazy kids having fun in a world that we were desperately trying to understand, and I often felt that I was on my own in trying to figure things out.

Eventually, our mothers separated from their abusive husbands, who weren't making the lives of their wives or their sons very pleasant. Benny would end up in Columbia, Maryland, while I would go to Oxon

Hill. We ran into one another once in the 90s when we were both in our early thirties. I was married with two children, and this was our first time seeing each other since we were kids.

A year or so after our reunion, during which we had enjoyed sharing memories of our turbulent youth, I was saddened to hear that my man Benny had overdosed. Benny's funeral was a heartbreaking experience, and it pushed me further on the path that I am currently on. Although he is no longer physically here with us, I still often think of my friend, and wish I had been better equipped back then to assist him in his life journey.

As I share these brief moments of our youth, I can almost feel the warmth of his spirit. When he laughed, Benny looked like a bowl of Jell-O; his entire body shook when expressing joy.

God bless the souls of Jerome Benny Etheridge, Steve Cornish, William Pierre Strong and Vance Boyd. You all played an important role in my life, and will never be forgotten. Until we meet again when I'm called home to gather in God's kingdom.

CHAPTER 10

REAPING BENEFITS FROM A NOT SO PLEASANT PAST

Boxing was once a big part of my life, and it helped build my confidence and self-discipline. During my short professional career, I remained on as a preliminary fighter, leading up the main and co-featured fights. Basically, this meant you must always be ready to fight at any given moment. In 1990, I got a call from matchmaker Cleveland Burgess to fill in and fight the young upcoming champion, Daryl "Too Sweet" Coley, who was making his professional debut. I had heard many good things about the amateur star, and I had nothing to lose.

Just before receiving the call, I was kicked back drinking a 40-ounce malt liquor, which I poured down the drain so to jump into focus. I began jockeying to be paid more money, seeing that I was a last-minute fill-in—or victim. Unlike most sports, boxing doesn't have one sanctioning body of rules. The D.C. boxing commission was barely paying a hundred dollars a round to put our lives on the line for entertainment. I got Mr. Burgess to break me off an extra hundred, though.

I stopped before the mirror and started shadowboxing to get

myself hyped and burn the beer out of my gut, then called my trainer. He was against me fighting, stating that I wouldn't win if I didn't knock him out. That said to me that he didn't think I could win.

I ignored his advice and headed uptown to Coolidge High School to compete. The fight was balanced for maybe a round or so, before his hand-speed became overwhelming. I started catching leather from all angles, and Daryl won a unanimous decision. He'd go on to have a fairly successful professional career, getting a title shot against the golden boy Oscar De La Hoya, who stopped him in seven.

Today I occasionally see Daryl, and we share a mutual respect for one another. He's currently training fighters, and I recently sent him a jokingly serious message about a rematch. I've been itching for a long time to step back into the ring to spar and feel that past warrior glory.

My problem was lacking in consistency, and the finger of blame points directly back at me. I lived as an abuser of drugs and alcohol as a means to escape the mental and emotional baggage I had been carrying from teenager to adult. Now with the ability to articulate my thoughts, writing has become my drug of choice. It helped me to slow down, relax, and enjoy life and know that everything is going to be alright.

Studies show that children who have witnessed and been the recipient of physical and verbal abuse display anxiety, depression, high levels of aggression and anti-social behavior that lingers into adulthood. I learned early on to feed off negativity, since that's all I received growing up. I was always trying to prove myself worthy of love, support and attention. Deep down, I knew my parents loved me, but their actions rarely showed it. As a child, my parents' marriage rarely seemed healthy for them or me.

I've come to realize the courage it took for my mother to finally pack up and start a new life on her own. She had three children, but actually, only me and my younger sister decided to live with our mother after the breakup. My younger brother, a top athlete in high school at that time, chose to stay with his father and continued in his athletic endeavors—which would ultimately win him a football scholarship.

Sharing these memories makes me think of how my brother may

have felt about being away from his mother, sister and his older brother. We never talked about this, but I'm certain he experienced some lonely moments. But, knowing him as I do, he likely pushed those feelings to the side, worked hard and practiced self-discipline, which helped him become a better all-around athlete. Those are also the benefits of being encouraged and supported to excel towards your absolute best.

Despite my brother and I being fairly close, we were A Tale of Two Brothers; one excels after being encouraged while the other is a drug abuser. I drank and smoked my trouble away for a temporary escape, and more often than not, I said "fuck it" because my fear-no-evil attitude made me feel loved and important. For a long time, I stayed angry at my mother, because we'd leave but she'd always come back. And that anger intensified knowing that I was being abused by a man who wasn't even my father.

In 1981, my mother mounted up the courage to finally leave her marriage for good and file for divorce. She, my sister and I would move to Oxon Hill, but before we moved, Jason, the master musician, came to live with our family.

Jason was the golden child of the Johnson side of the family, while Jeff served the same purpose on the Chapman side. I felt that I was seen as the big dummy—an opinion often repeated to me by the men of the family.

Jason and I had a heated rivalry, and I always felt like he got a kick out of putting me down. I took it personally, being already emotionally damaged, so it didn't take much to get me heated. But still, we did everything together. He kept me up on what was hip, as I despised being considered a country boy who once lived in an area affectionately known as Dog Patch. When Jason stayed with us, I'd tag along with him going to his band practices. We'd catch a bus there, and the band's manager would drive us home—which demonstrated Jason's value as a musician. I was his sidekick, and being there eventually got me my first set of conga drums.

I had first gotten interested in congas when I saw Trouble Funk in the 80s and T-Bone, the conga player. There was something culturally authentic in watching him smack those drums while wearing a dashiki, and I guess you can say I was hooked.

The Regulation Band was the name of Jason's band, and they were on a much lower level, performing at schools and rec centers. I'd accompany Jason to practice and found myself constantly watching their conga player, a guy known as Scooby. I had never played congas before, but when the band took breaks, I'd go on stage and try mimicking what I saw him doing. In time, Scoob noticed his influence and ended up giving me his drums. Surprised and thrilled, I accepted the drums, although they were beat up, scratched up and cracked up.

Fast forward to 2011. I'm remarried, living in the area where the Regulation Band once practiced and performed, when I recognized Scoob after so many years—on the streets begging me for money. I had heard he was homeless, and I could tell that he had no idea who I was. I asked if he remembered Jason, and he said he did. So I told the story of me being his cousin who'd accompanied him, and how he gave me my first set of congas. I could tell that he didn't remember, but he went along with it and repeated what I had said to his homeless friends. I embraced him and gave him five dollars, and I could tell he was appreciative.

Now, flashing back on those days, I'm excited to get me some Elmer's glue and seal the cracks in the drums…

My on the job training in becoming a drummer began when all the fellas came by. Vance, Mo, Chuck and Pierre came over and found some buckets and cans to give me a rhythm, and Hollywood started being groomed in my basement of our neighborhood junkyard band.

In our minds, we were cranking—until my poppa came home and raised a whole lot of fuss.

"Got dammit! Stop all that bang, bang, bang noise!" And like clockwork, he'd locate me and kick my already ragged drums to the floor. We'd scramble like roaches when the lights came on, getting out of the house, still high and laughing.

Usually, crazy Maurice would start mocking my father in his best imitation. "George, come up in here! I'll run everybody out da got dam house. I don't give ah-dam who child you is… just talkin' shit!"

We'd all be laughing and go hang out at someone else's home or go to the park. Other Black families began to move into this predominately White middle-class community in the late 70s. Our family moved there around 1974, and the first guy I met was Big Benny, who became my best friend. I eventually met the rest of the guys, including the neighborhood bully Danny De Walt, who I'd eventually dethrone as the toughest dude in the neighborhood simply by standing up to him.

I was around fourteen, and we were on the bus coming home from school. I normally tried staying clear of Danny, but on this particular day, for whatever reason, he came my way. I've never been able to back down from a fight, despite Danny being nearly two hundred pounds or more to my maybe one-thirty. He started to taunt me. I was trembling like a leaf, but always ready to do battle. The shit I dealt with daily in my home had built my courage, especially against the bigger guys—like my pop.

We got off the bus, Danny looking fierce and stepping to me aggressively. I began to mimic Ali, floating like a butterfly, staying on the outside and flicking jabs. Some landed, but they had little sting against this big dude, and they likely irritated more than they hurt. Danny lowered his head and did a bull rush, overpowering me with an overhand right that landed square on my nose. Blood gushing, I kept fighting.

Danny saw this and didn't want to hurt me any more than he already had. He tried consoling me with, "Come on, man, D, chill."

I kept swinging. Though truth be told, it was mostly drama because I was glad he no longer wanted to throw another mighty blow. Danny eventually walked away.

The next day at school, I'm hearing the word on the street of me kicking Danny's ass. Okay, I'll take it. I didn't even try to dispute this fabricated truth. In thinking back, I'm certain this false rumor was due to me being the first to stand up to him, and eventually we became cool.

Thinking back to the band. They needed a conga player, and since I now had the drums, I became Scooby's replacement. Jason or rather, Horny Jay, (he played trumpet) convinced his band members to allow me to practice and eventually play with the band. The name Hollywood fit well, because I couldn't play as well as I made it look. I was a real showman, dancing my ass off while grooving the pocket. I loved the feeling that I was becoming somebody without fighting, so I just embraced the love in this new environment.

But eventually, I begin to fully focus on boxing instead. A moment that was big for me in my evolution occurred in my early years, in 1980, when I was being a bully to a brother who was cool with Chuck and Mo. For whatever reason, I didn't like him. He'd take all my insults and just walk away, which was a sign of his maturity in comparison to mine. I never put my hands on him. Years later, we'd run into each other, sometimes hang out, laugh and have fun. We got to know each other, and I came to the conclusion that we had both been dealing with the same type of dysfunction at home. My inner self started feeling guilty every time I saw him, because I could never answer to myself why I had picked on him so much.

One day, out of the blue, I looked him in the eye and said, "Brother, I'm sorry for the many years of trying to humiliate you. Or as we'd say back then… punk you out."

He paused for a moment, looking caught off guard, and in his typical, I'm-hard-forget-that-soft-shit-fashion, said, "Come on, man, we good. We was kids back then. It ain't no thing."

"Naw, man," I replied. "It is something to me, and it's eating me up on the inside of how wrong I was."

He finally accepted my apology, and we embraced and have been cool ever since.

As a young man, I was very reckless, but I could not or would not show that it was due to me hurting within. To me, respect was gained by showing no fear of standing up to anything or anybody. This made me feel like I was somebody, and that only I was aware of my low self-esteem.

In the early years of my boxing, I had gotten to know two very talented fighters, and the three of us became friends at the Hillcrest Heights Boxing center. Both of them had tremendous ability, and both would end up dying in the ring.

John "Tippy" Gordon and I were fairly close. We were also classmates at Oxon Hill Senior High. I had joined the Marines a year or so before his death, and when I heard about it, I was heartbroken. I got more information from his former high school sweetheart, who shared with me how Tippy would tell her, "Hollywood like you." But out of respect for him, I never pursued her until years later. She said it was one of the things that John admired about me. John collapsed in the ring while sparring and died en route to the hospital on September 24th, 1984. God bless his soul.

The other boxer died in the ring the following year, in 1985, just as I'd become an All-Marine boxer. At that time, my unbalanced emotions continued to resurface, and there were times I hoped to be the next boxer to die inside the ring. But to God be the glory in recognizing my value. God doesn't make junk.

We've all experienced various ups and downs in life, and this body of work is meant to inspire anyone who may be suffering, a universal problem that transcends race, gender, lifestyle or religion. But we as Black people, in particular, are forced to continually adjust to the unjust, racist society in which we live, and this sometimes makes our challenge much easier said than actually done. But it can be and must be done.

We are a people of perseverance, and collectively we must be gentler in understanding our common Black struggle. It has manifested within all of us a sense of mental disorder, and like everything, some deal with it better than others. As a young man, I was very much a product of my emotionally unstable, violent environment. I tried to give the outer impression of never being afraid, though I was always afraid within.

As I got older, fresh out of the Marines and battling depression, drinking and smoking weed was my escape. I remember many times bawling in tears, feeling that I no longer wanted to live. It wasn't until I wandered into Inner Visions and became a part of The Gathering of Men, a spiritually based men's support group, that I began to open up and share my burdens. I began to feel trust. I had no idea of how to constructively channel my inner rage and anger until I discovered my truth by way of writing. Writing helped me discover my dreams, which I've come to interpret as God's way of reminding us that we can do whatever our heart desires, but it requires faith and hard work to succeed.

I'll conclude by saying that it's better to have learned late than never. I am grateful for the time spent in boxing and my many experiences. Despite never reaching my full potential, boxing allowed me to travel and meet wonderful people both in and outside the ring. It also helped me to better understand life and my place in it, and ultimately, I learned that God had another plan for me.

Boxing certainly served its purpose. I am no longer a competitor in the ring, but boxing is still very much a part of my life. I still train as if I'm an active fighter, and I now channel this energy towards being the best that life has to offer.

So I encourage you to make that drastic change and start a revolution inside your mind. Recognize your own evolution and grow from it by returning to what brought all of us into being… love and God.

Conscientious efforts are needed in order to be more loving towards one another—angry people cannot create a peaceful planet.

CHAPTER 11

POST-TRAUMATIC SYNDROME AND BLACK HEALTH

The Black experience varies, and contrary to stereotypical belief, we're very diverse as a people. However, one common denominator of being Black in America is that we've all experienced hatred, discrimination and injustice. This adds to the burden that all people face in the journey called life, and different people have different responses to it.

Mental health conditions don't discriminate, and anyone can experience the challenges of mental illness. However, how you cope with these conditions may differ. According to the Health and Human Services Office of Minority Health, Black people are ten percent more likely to experience severe psychological conditions due to exclusions in health, education, social and economic resources. This is in addition to the historical horrors of slavery, race-based exclusion, injustice, poverty, and racial profiling, all of which have had lingering effects on our mental well-being and stability. We should not be afraid to ask for help if we need it.

I speak from my own experience of needing help, but instead turning to the self-medication of drugs, alcohol and isolation. During that time, I was wearing a mask to give the impression that everything was fine, rather than seek help for my depression and anxiety. Masking pain is still a big problem amongst men. I've been there, and I hope to encourage others to move beyond this stigma of admitting pain and commence to get a checkup from the neck up. Our mental health can no longer be ignored.

I recall when I was convinced to see a therapist after moving beyond my self-imposed barrier, convincing myself that I wasn't crazy and "dam sho wasn't weak." In time, I realized it was beneficial, and now I'm all-in as an advocate of mental stability. I can only imagine what my father, his father and countless other African Americans must have endured during a blatantly cruel, racially unjust society. I'd venture to say there was no mental or emotional assistance. And even if there were institutions or groups that catered to the needs of Black people, many didn't seek help due to a self-imposed stigma. Still, that turmoil faced by African Americans also demonstrates an excellent example of our Black perseverance.

My father who raised me was born in the year 1938 and served his country in the Army in the late 1950s. He met my mother, who had a two-year-old son (me), and they married in 1965. Then he began the task of raising and teaching two boys how to survive and be a man in a country where the killing of Black people, especially then but even so now, was deemed justifiable. Our tragic and unjust history is full of death along with a long list of modern-day unjust killings: Trayvon Martin, Eric Garner, Tamir Rice, George Floyd—the list goes on and on.

Many have tried to destroy our stability, but with faith, perseverance and persistence, we remain empowered. Hopefully, society will one day see that strength lies in our differences as opposed to similarities.

It was once said by the former First Lady and humanitarian Eleanor Roosevelt, "No one can make you feel inferior without your consent." Although I agree with the quote, white people will never quite understand the mental and emotional burden that we're still forced to carry and overcome in a society that continues to benefit from the lingering effects of an inhumane past.

I have read about cellular memory, which proves that traumatic memories stored in individual cells outside the brain can be passed on from parent to offspring or from generation to generation. Time does not heal all wounds; rather, they maintain their existence in what science calls our cellular memory. Every cell in our bodies holds hundreds of pages of information on all levels of our being, physically, emotionally, mentally and spiritually. It's constantly updated from your past and up until our present moments. Scientists believe these cellular memories might mean the difference between a healthy life and illnesses, including cancer. But replacing those bad memories with good ones may provide one of the most powerful ways of curing illness.

I'd now like to address a major problem that stems from racial profiling. Consider police interaction in the investigation of White crime in comparison to Black crime. Check the statistics: typically, we serve more time in prison for the same crime as compared to our White counterparts, who usually live to speak about the ordeal.

My younger brother and I are both very passionate, especially when it comes to serving. He, too, is a former Marine as well as a long-time veteran in law enforcement, and we've spent many years bickering about police misconduct. The way we get through it is by reminding each other about listening, as opposed to trying to convince the other. But we found common ground concerning the unquestionable guilt of the officers involved in the murders of twelve-year-old Tamir Rice and Eric Garner, both of which in his words made him feel a sense of shame that the bad apples involved made the whole police force look rotten. This has been my argument all along: the need for leadership to take down the blue wall of protection, regardless of the circumstances. It is no wonder that we, the Black community who bear witness to blatant injustice, want to simply say, "Fuck da police."

I'm not saying that my brother has lost faith in his profession, but he's aware of and respects my perspective. In turn, I've come to better understand from the view of an officer. I recall him telling me stories of how he'd have to go into the Black community to investigate, where he would be bombarded with insults and rants of "Uncle Tom"—a derogatory term used to belittle the Black man as a sellout.

After research, however, I discovered that Josiah Henson, the inspiration behind author Harriet Beecher Stowe's book *Uncle Tom's Cabin* published in 1852, was more a hero than sellout. He endured countless beatings, especially as a child for learning to read. As an adult, he had great physical strength and leadership ability. Eventually, he became a master chief marketer, selling farm produce. While doing so, he rubbed shoulders with eminent lawyers and businessmen and learned the skills of running a business. He became a great preacher who eventually raised money to purchase his freedom, only to be manipulated into losing it again. In 1830, Henson, his wife and two children escaped slavery and fled to Canada, and in 1841 he helped start a freeman settlement, which became a final stop on the Underground Railroad.

Wow. Information is power, and sadly this misconception of Uncle Tom continues today. Sadly, I can almost envision blacks hating on one another for using opportunities that were given to them regardless of the circumstances. Hating on a man for trying to better himself so to be in a position to help others. Now, I think a little deeper before speaking and calling another Black man Uncle Tom.

My brother often reminds me of Black-on-Black crime, and how long are we going to blame the White man? I agree, despite knowing the source of it: racism White supremacy, which is as American as apple pie. I'm no armchair revolutionary, and I will continue to do my part to counter injustice and work on behalf of improving upon our post-traumatic syndrome.

My brother once stated that he thought I would make a good officer. He said law enforcement needs brothers like me. My response was I wouldn't, because being too Black and conscious makes both Black and White, uncomfortable. I'd be a target, and there is no way that I'd hide who I am as a loving Black man who wears his culture proudly. That's a lesson I learned firsthand after six years of military service and my refusal to submit to being a little less Black.

My heart is full of forgiveness, but as mentioned, to forgive does not mean that you forget.

My rough upbringing, in my opinion, was simply looked upon as a way of making me tough. But there existed no balance, meaning you can't tear down without lifting up. What I'm learning, especially now in sharing my journey, is to give myself credit for my evolution in growth. I no longer feel the shame of the boy who sometimes still cries inside of the man. I have no fear of appearing vulnerable; we all have vulnerabilities. The old me has died, but through God's grace, I've been reborn into a new person seeking to achieve the greatness that God has bestowed upon me.

Brother Malcolm once stated that we must first engage in a revolution of the mind. Once this begins to happen, other things will follow. This will lead to not only the liberation of Black people, but also the liberation of this nation. Then and only then, as spoken by Dr. King, can all of God's creation be able to join hands together and sing that ole Negro spiritual of free at last, free at last, thank God almighty that we are finally free at last.

Love is revolutionary.

CHAPTER 12

BREAKING THE CHAINS OF CULTURAL CONFORMITY BASED ON HIS-STORY

Most of us are seeking to find and be who we really are. Finding yourself is not like discovering a hundred-dollar bill in the pocket of a jacket you haven't worn in quite some time. Your true self is buried beneath layers of cultural conditioning and other people's opinions.

Knowing and being not afraid to display your true self is the beginning of all wisdom. I remain on the path of finding, recreating and discovering different aspects of me. I've learned to fall in love with the reflection I see in the mirror. No longer do I feel shame in admitting that I didn't always feel this way. Although the rising sun dispels the darkness of night, it cannot remove the darkness of my skin, and how I am met with racism, injustice, hatred and terror. This treatment can create an internal conflict of self-hatred that can grow inside like cancer. This tragic cycle is partially due to people of color being force-fed what I like to call his-story instead of a balanced study of the contribution of all human beings.

Books by historians such as Dr. Ivan Van Sertima, author of *The African Presence in Ancient America; They Came before Columbus* or Dr. Chancellor Williams, who wrote *The Destruction of Black Civilization* are just a few that can inform us about striving Black civilizations. I will continue to meet such resistance head-on as I learn how race and racial inequality have shaped American history from its beginnings, but it only takes a little kindness to change the human heart. I challenge all comers who equate being kind to being weak in attempting to change the course of humanity.

We are deeply profound social creatures. We share rich social qualities with many other species, forming families like mammals and cooperating at large scales in ways that are similar to ants and bees. Where we seem to differ is in our ability to build upon cultural information, such as one group feeling threatened by another, in both a conscious and unconscious way. Psychiatrist Frantz Fanon, the author of *Black Skin, White Mask*, argues that colonialism has corrupted people's understanding of themselves. Black people have an image of self that is distorted, a negative image constructed by White colonizers.

Now, some may say, "Oh, here we go again. Blame the White man." But that is not the truth. What I am saying is, when you study the history, contribution and perseverance of Black people, you become empowered.

There is nothing threatening about confessing the beauty of our Blackness that dismisses the myth that we've been fed. My birthplace is planet Earth, my race is human, my political affiliation is freedom, and my religion is love. I'm bold and self-assured, with no interest in the so-called normal standards set by the White culture, a culture that conquered, raped, enslaved and terrorized. Chains no longer exist around bodies, but minds are still colonized.

I've heard elders speak about a time, not so long ago, when some of our people were suspicious of being called Black. We're all well aware of how we have transformed from being Niggers, Negro, Colored, Black and now African American. It's been a long, challenging journey, and it's time to engage in the process of decolonizing our mind and loving the beauty of our Blackness.

I once recall my sister introducing me to a female friend by saying, "This is big brother, Darrick, and he's into all that Black stuff."

Caught off guard, I replied, "What do you mean by that? Aren't you Black, and what is that Black stuff?"

Recognizing the self-hatred unconsciously spread amongst us, I've concluded this to be a part of the chain that must be broken in our cultural conditioning. In paraphrasing Malcolm, we live amongst a society with a media that is the most powerful entity here on Earth. It conditions us to believe who we should love and who to hate.

Black people are often overlooked in the field of mental health. For me, seeking help through counsel helped me push through the societal misconceptions. A therapist I saw in the mid-1990s helped lead me to various community-based groups specializing in mental, emotional and spiritual uplift, all of which built confidence with the beauty of my Blackness.

I recall some years ago, a young lady politely excused herself and said, "Brother, no offense, but every time I see you, I'm suddenly filled with pride. You remind me of a Black Panther."

A smile came across my face, and I thought, Wow! Why would I be offended?

The late John Henrik Clarke speaks of how Black people must honor our roots, the enslaved Africans whose shoulders we stand on that created us: the African American tree. Powerful people cannot afford to be educated by the people who once oppressed them, because once you are truly educated, you will not ask for power. You take it!

The most significant thing for me in my six years of military service was ultimately learning that information is power. It was our misfortune that made America wealthy; slavery built the system of U.S. capitalism. This issue has been revisited time and time again by leading civil rights activists. The Reverend Dr. Martin Luther King, Jr. stated that America has written a check to the American Negro that has come back marked 'insufficient funds.' He called instead for " …a check that will give us upon demand the riches of freedom and security of justice."

Supreme Court Justice Sonia Sotomayor once said, "It is important for all of us to appreciate where we come from and how that history has really shaped us in ways that we might not understand."

So we must continue to evolve by drastically changing our thinking. I say Revolution.

CHAPTER 13

Radical Transformation

I remember I once felt inclined to quit school after hearing my father say to my mother, "Let dat boy-ah drop out of school and get a job, he ain't learning a dam thang."

She quickly responded, "I don't care if that boy is twenty years old, he gon' get his high school diploma."

And that I did, despite the embarrassment I felt during and leading up to me eventually graduating. It was also a new beginning, especially for my mother, who finally said enough is enough of the abuse and we left for good.

Before graduation, I had been working and doing fairly well in retail, but after graduation, I wanted more. College was certainly not an option, because I barely got through high school. Although I started practicing boxing in 1980, I had never given any serious thought to becoming a professional, and my future was uncertain. Although I had landed there, I don't recall any real aspiration in being a Marine, other than having an uncle and cousin who were both Marines. They'd shared a few things with me, and their reputation of being the toughest branch of the military appealed to me.

I'd wandered into the USMC recruiter office, which was located not far from where I trained as a boxer, and met a recruiter. When he learned that I was a fighter, he had his strategy laid out to get me to sign the dotted line. He gave me the history of former All-Marine Corps boxers who went on to fame as professionals. That drew my interest and now I had a plan of joining and trying out for the All-Marine Corps boxing team. So in June of 1984, I took off to Paris Island for boot camp. I'll never forget my mother telling me just before going, "You ain't got nothing to worry about. You been raised by George Chapman, and I guarantee you ain't no Marine tougher than he!"

After boot camp, I'd attend Motor Transport School as a heavy equipment operator, and shortly after, I got word of the All-Marine Corps boxing championship. It was the determining factor behind choosing the 1984 All-Marine boxing team, so I entered. I loved boxing, but truth be told, I had no real passion for pursuing the sport; it was simply something that I did and happened to be pretty good at when focused.

This lack of passion was made clear in the first round of competition, when I was beaten. I can't say I showed any real potential, and came away more embarrassed than anything, due to the front page of the base newspaper covering the All-Marine Boxing Tournament with a picture of me leaning way back on the ropes and my opponent's right hand cocked and going in for the kill.

I'd lost a unanimous decision and didn't feel I had done enough to be considered for the team. Then, I remembered hearing about an open-door policy. You could come into the snake pit, where the All-Marine team trained, and challenge for a spot on the team. So I did, and I destroyed the guy. He was a Washingtonian like me, but I took no pity. I crushed him and got a slot on the team, and accomplished my goal in joining.

Just as I was starting to gain a little ground in my first year as an All-Marine boxer, I was suddenly sent to Okinawa and Mainland Japan in 1986. This is when real change started to come about in my life, as I discovered the joy of reading, which helped reveal a greater sense of cultural pride in me. Throughout my Far East tour of duty, I read countless stories of Black perseverance. Upon arriving in Okinawa, Japan, I recall meeting cats from the windy city of Chicago who engaged me a little deeper in our history and culture. I learned about the significant impact of their homeboy Fred Hampton, a young, charismatic revolutionary who served as the chairman of the Chicago chapter of the Black Panther Party. He had an amazing ability to bring people together, transcending racial barriers—an ability that generated fear in our U.S. government. They saw Fred had helped expand the movement beyond being simply Black, rather he was able to inspire oppressed people of various cultures.

Ultimately, Fred would be assassinated by the Chicago police department following the lead of our government and the racist ideology of John Edgar Hoover. He had declared the BPP a threat to national security, basically giving the green light to police agencies throughout the country that it was open season on killing Panthers. On December 4, 1969, the Chicago Police Department and the FBI raided the office in the wee hours of the morning. It was later discovered that the officers followed a map drawn by an informant that led them straight to Fred's room, where he was shot to death while lying in bed.

There was no attempt to capture Fred alive. Instead, he lay helpless in bed and was shot to death as he slept. He had committed no crime other than being viewed as a threat. No one was ever convicted of this crime, but the city paid off the family in a wrongful death suit.

I also learned of the ties between Fred Hampton's family and that of brutally slain civil rights martyr Emmitt Till, whose gruesome remains were on display for the world to see at the request of his mother. She had demanded an open casket so the world could bear witness to the racist hate and the vicious terror cast upon even a fourteen-year-old boy. The remains of Emmitt's mangled body were on display in newspapers and magazines around the world, tapping into the moral unconsciousness of America. It was also yet another example in a long list of ugly reminders that in America, "Black lives don't appear to matter."

The culprits who brutally killed a child walked free after being acquitted by an all-white jury and later sold rights to the truth of them killing Emmitt to *Life Magazine* without repercussion under the law of double jeopardy. After Emmitt's brutal murder, the civil rights movement slowly soared to new heights in the fight for justice, equal rights and opportunity for Blacks in America. Sadly, this fight still rages.

I've come to view whatever challenge I may face as nothing more than a building block that will continue to help me to grow. In my own growth, I recognize that I've been in several seasons of development, because every day is a new day of us enjoying God's mercy. So, in turn, I exercise my gratitude, reach for the sky and keep myself prepared for new beginnings.

I've lived and I've learned through the course of my journey. I've accepted that you can't keep looking back, dwelling on the wrongs.

I believe we're either in the process of resisting God's truth or being shaped and molded by his spirit. I stake claim to the latter in knowing that we have been made in his image. Buddhism teaches that we are shaped by our thoughts, and we become that which we think. So when the mind is pure and filled with positivity, joy follows like a shadow that never leaves. My aim is to keep that shadow of joy by my side, shining atop my entire being.

The power of forgiveness does not mean that you forget. It means you stop allowing yourself to be a prisoner. There can be no peace without forgiveness, and there is nothing weak about it. In contrast, anger and resentment ultimately bring you down and make reaching your ultimate purpose that much more difficult. The road towards being a better person is always under construction, and I am happy with my own self-improvement as I keep on pushing with an open mind, guided by our heavenly father.

I now come to grips with not questioning or doubting anything about my truth. I am only delighted to be steadily learning and giving voice to my once silent soul as I seek and find a greater sense of freedom. So I say to you, the reader, to move beyond your feelings of anger and blame. Recognize and be present, because the power lies within you to create joy and true happiness.

By being a diligent reader who tries to maintain an open mind, I've discovered the beauty of me. I release and let go by way of baring my soul through writing, and I continue to do my best to improve in the process of being a good listener. I've learned to slow the mental motor of my mind, which taps the brakes of my mouth and creates space for others to join in and be a part of whatever is being discussed. In doing so, I become more informed by hearing a different perspective.

Fellow visionaries like me truly understand the therapeutic effect of writing. I've learned to use pain and disappointment as motivation when things go wrong. I try to remain open as opposed to blaming in the hope of discovering the lesson, which may require digging a little deeper.

I am reminded of a poem written by a very influential poet, Ms. Abeona Walker, titled, "Will there ever be a time?" She conducted some workshops that inspired me to write poetry as I was enduring the heartache of officially ending my marriage. This particular poem spoke so clearly to me that I mentally claimed it as my own. Many years later, I shared it with Ms. Walker, who was so moved and honored in me sharing how the poem was part of my healing.

One line from the poem states: 'When will our relationship be about relating, rather than a battleship of strategies and maneuvers, where honesty is never the best policy? Can't you just accept yourself, so maybe you can then accept me? Then we can trust, respect and believe one another, you liking and honoring my many strengths as opposed to blowing up my few weaknesses. Will there ever come a time?"

I've since begun developing a closer relationship with our heavenly father, and in doing so, I've found the courage to endure the penetrating pain of self-discovery. It continues to reveal the ugly sides of me, and not doing so only prevents the manifestation of my absolute best. I'd venture to say that we all want the best of who we are to shine bright. Sometimes it seems that our efforts in striving towards our betterment as people are too hard, but we have to keep on pushing.

Despite the chaos I was born into, never did I stop believing in myself and feeling that there was something special about me and my life. Often I feel as if I'm going in circles, which can bring forth moments of doubt if I were to allow it. But my increased faith helps me overcome this aspect of fear that was holding me back.

No longer can we allow ourselves to be trapped inside the prison of our minds. I continue in my efforts to break those chains of cultural conditioning and distorted perceptions based on stereotypes. I now take pride in displaying my best values: dependability, character, work ethic and being a more considerate person who cares about the well-being of humanity.

"Let us all hope that the dark clouds of racial prejudice will soon pass away and the deep fog of misunderstanding will be lifted from our fear-drenched communities, and in some not too distant tomorrow the radiant stars of love and brotherhood will shine over our great nation with all their scintillating beauty."

— Martin Luther King Jr., Letter from the Birmingham Jail

CHAPTER 14

AMERICA HAS YET TO REACH GREATNESS

The African American never can be blamed for his patriotic animosity. He's only reacting to four hundred years of conscious racism by American whites.

"Racism is like a Cadillac—they come out with a new version every year." - Malcolm X

Racism is nothing more than fear and ignorance. It's sad to see how this ugliness continues to slowly destroy our world: a world where narrow-minded individuals still resist the reality that all people desire the same sense of happiness and security. Lynchings were used as a common form of hate in the early 1900s, especially down south with groups such as the Black Legion and Ku Klux Klan. Today, with so many unjust killings of unarmed people of color, we now have the Blue Klux Klan. Deputized law enforcement officers have replaced the white-hooded sheets. Now, some wear business suits, carry briefcases, wear black robes and occupy powerful places in making decisions in the direction of this country.

After serving as a U.S. Marine, I developed a passion to serve my community. I recall being a participant of the Enough is Enough Movement. Its goal was to re-open the police shooting that killed Archie Elliot, an unarmed Black man from District Heights, Maryland. He was pulled over for driving under the influence, wearing only short pants and no shirt after ending his shift as a construction worker on a hot summer day. He was then placed in the front seat of a police cruiser, strapped in by the seat belt. Moments later, officers claimed he was pointing a gun and opened fire, killing Archie instantly. Logic says, however, that when he was told to step out of the vehicle, according to police procedure, he would have been searched for weapons or anything illegal. And, in wearing only shorts, logic says a weapon would easily be found.

Unfortunately, this story is all too familiar throughout our country, and more often than not, the officers walk free with no charges against them. And some wonder still about the distrust between police and the African American community.

Written in honor of Michael Brown and the countless number of Black men and women unjustly killed by the hand of law enforcement—

"Hands up," I thought, was a universal language meaning surrender?

Regardless of what may have occurred prior... "But then again" when speak-in of being Black in

the American unjust system, historically speak-in, my skin, in the eyes of "some" is seen as a treat, our word less creditable "No" matter how many witnessed a young man fleeing police "when suddenly"

He's struck by a bullet and its impact jolts him around, hands reaching for the sky, no weapon

Pleading "don't shoot," and the distance between suspect and police makes you wonder "how"

Did he pose such a treat, thus causing the officer to keep on shooting... bullets rip-in through flesh, as the life of yet another Black child isn't afforded a second chance.

I recall the bitter feelings after transitioning from military to civilian life, basically forced out of the military with other than honorable discharge, but in my mind, it was due to me being too bold, too cool, self-assured and too dam Black!

My militancy was on the rise due to having discovered the joy of reading and better understanding history, while at the same time decolonizing my mind of all the half-truths and lies based on the his-story still being taught in the American educational system. I gained a greater sense of self-confidence as I remained in the process of better loving and educating myself. A Man who stood up like a man, unafraid to think critically outside of the societal box.

My last three years of military service had me stationed at Henderson Hall in Arlington, outside of my Prince George County home. Since I was basically stationed at home, my military mind began to fade. I was developing a higher level of consciousness, which is key to growth. I am grateful to be able to share this part of my journey, when Crack was king and D.C. was known as Dodge City. Our mayor for life was entrapped by a major government sting—yeah, Marion Barry liked to party. I recall seeing him at a few clubs, as well in attendance for local boxing. In fact, he sponsored the D.C. Mayor's Cup, a popular amateur boxing tournament that I recall once winning.

"Dam D, your mayor is a crackhead," I'd often hear from everybody outside of the DMV. And if you aren't black, you'll never understand the burden we feel when things like this happen. It stems from America's long history of devaluing, demonizing, degrading, unjustly killing and incarcerating Black people ever since we were forcefully brought to these shores in chains. Barry wasn't laundering money, but a lot of taxpayers' cash was spent to bring him down. This is why after his legal matters, we voted him right back into office.

I hung out at all the hot spots throughout the city, and recall often turning on the local news the next morning and hearing about a shooting at the club where I had partied.

I lived multiple lives in the 1980s as a U.S. Marine, boxer, club-hopping drunk, pothead, ladies' man and part-time bouncer in a Spanish club in downtown D.C. There, I worked security under the leadership of a crazy

Marine who preferred intimidation. And if that didn't work, then he wanted me to beat people up, knowing that I was a boxer.

His unprofessionalism caused this job to be increasingly dangerous. He was a hot-head, and one night the crowd exploded, and the police had to be called to escort us out to our cars. His was vandalized, and after that, I quit.

Despite my double life, my consciousness was still rising. I would attend several cultural events throughout the city. I saw Minister Farrakhan speak, and the thing I remember most when passing the word around base was the fear of the Brotherman towards the other man. They condemned the minister as a hate teacher, just the same as I viewed Rush Limbaugh. The point is based on individual interpretation, and standing up kept me in trouble. I refuse to submit to a slave mentality, listening to others trying to convince us of who to love and who to hate.

A moment that led to my Marine Corps demise occurred between me and a punk, redneck sergeant on an evening when I'm about to get off duty. I'm dropping off a package at the military police headquarters when a big, good ole boy somewhere around 6'3" gives a hard glare. I said nothing and attempted to keep it moving, causing him to reply that I better respect his stripes.

I respond, "Excuse me, but shouldn't we first respect each other as men?"

I ended up in the base commander's office with an insubordination charge, but in my mind, the charge was my bold confidence towards his racist demeanor. They commence trying to assassinate my character by pulling out my spotty military records. The worse offense was me taking advantage of a Japanese cab driver, who offered my partner and me a free ride to buy him a twelve-pack of beer, which was illegal for them to purchase. We agreed, and the military police take notice. I go over and explain it was common practice in the Marines, but the MPs are not having it, and we're charged with bootlegging. I get busted and lose rank, another BS reminder that I was sick of military service.

In 1988, I was the only Marine of five to advance beyond the first round of completion in the Olympic trials. When I got back to base, I was hailed a hero and made the front-page news in the base paper. I recall family and friends who worked for the Department of Defense calling my mother to send me words of praise and congratulations. That wore off, though, when an officer called me "boy" in the middle of the chow hall, reminding me that in their eyes, I was simply a non-compliant nigger.

I was bitter, and quickly got a job that I got tired of just as quick, due to being over-worked and under-paid. This scenario repeated itself with three different companies in six years before settling with one that kept me satisfied for the next seven, when I found a job as a delivery truck driver for a print shop.

I'll never forget the aftermath of the tragic events of 9/11, everyone eager to display their patriotism by donning the American flag. Sales went up due to demand, but there was no conforming me, an angry Black man. I compared what was new to White America to the history of terror in our Black reality of dealing with them!

I was allowed to drive the company van home after work, and placed a red, black and green flag of Black liberation on the antenna. I'll never forget the look of pride I received from some of the Blacks, reading their expressions of "Right on, Brother." In contrast, others, both Black and White, gave a look that carried the words of comedian genius Richard Pryor: "That nigger crazy."

My transformation, or rather, evolution in becoming a much better person started with one day wandering around downtown when I stumbled upon The Inner Visions Spiritual Life Institute. I've mentioned this place before, as it had a big impact on my development.

Inner Visions helped me to recognize the need to first fix me. This was the beginning of my mission of fixing my life, with hopes of changing the world. I started to attend a program called Men on the Move, and its lead facilitator, Mr. Adeyemi Bandelle, who was then married to Ms. Vanzant, saw things in me that I didn't see in myself.

I soon became a regular participant, and before long, I found myself as a facilitator. My nerves were racing, but I was able to push through, and in time my confidence was built. So much so, in fact, that Adeyemi chose me as a co-host on his radio broadcast. I'd sit there in the studio looking the part of radio host with headphones on and microphone before me, but basically, I was sitting there in silence, listening. I didn't say much on the show unless it was something asked of me.

I recall what became a very significant moment as we traveled to Harlem to gather with the brothers there, trying to create a movement of Men being better leaders, brothers, lovers and friends. It was during the Harlem gathering that I realized I wasn't alone in Men carrying baggage due to the absence, abuse or lack of support from fathers. Here were grown men, not blaming but rather acknowledging our unconscious negative behaviors that generated from our fathers' negative energy.

I began sharing my discontent when a brother interjects and says, "Excuse me." As the group's focus turns toward him, he says, "Look at where you are, brother. Currently getting in tune with your inner spirit to become a better man. I'm certain that you're much further along spiritually than your father and most men of his generation. Trust me, I can relate to your animosity, but the difference between you and me is that you can change your situation, whereas I can only wish I had been able to generate the courage to at least make an attempt to forgive my father, who is no longer here amongst the living. So, brother, don't wait in trying to bridge that gap, in thinking that it's their responsibility to take the lead or make the first step. Forgive your father, you'll benefit in the future."

His advice would ultimately change my life by giving me the courage to talk to my father. I had to move beyond expectations as my emotions took the lead. I spoke my piece to my dad, and his response was, "Yeah, Darrick, I know. Chill out, I don't want the boys to hear." (His friends were not far away, drinking.)

"Fuck the boys," was my response, my anger nearly reaching its boiling point.

In looking back, I wondered what made me think he might embrace me and say, "Son, I'm sorry." Instead, he got embarrassed and I got mad.

At the next gathering, I couldn't wait to share the disappointment I'd felt. Everyone listened carefully, and before anyone spoke, Adeyemi simply said to me, "Brother, you can't have expectations of how the person should respond. Look at how many of us still struggle in dealing with our emotions. Forgiveness is for you, not the other person. It's a process, not an event, but me speaking my truth planted the seed to forgive."

Whereas today I am better equipped to manage and balance my emotions, by no means do I claim to be an expert in psychology or human behavior. Instead, the thoughts shared here are simply my views based on my own life experiences. These truths have freed me from the depths of where I was, and to God be the glory for the beauty in discovering who and where I am in my journey called life. I am creatively doing my part to make a difference in our world, and it's worth repeating that angry people cannot create a peaceful planet. I seek to do my part in the name of love.

I am a revolutionary who knows enlightenment comes in making the right choice, but in the end, our choices make us. We're free to choose our path, but we can't choose the consequences that come with them. Happiness is a choice, as is kindness, sadness or anger. So whatever choice you make, choose wisely.

My journey has been about living a more fulfilling life, starting every day by giving thanks for the breath that sustains me—God's reminder that he is ever-present.

I received a wonderful compliment from my oldest daughter while celebrating my fifty-seventh birthday.

She said, "I'm so proud of you. Many people who get older become grumpy, whereas you're more cheerful and not always so serious."

Her younger sister agreed, which reminded me of her saying to me many years ago, "Daddy, why are you so serious all the time?"

The difference is, now I choose to allow God's light to shine through me in the never-ending process of self-discovery. Honoring the creative force of our lives enables us to accomplish our goals based on decisions rather than conditions.

It's my hope that you enjoyed my creative journey, and are inspired to maximize your own.

–One Luv-

EPILOGUE

CHANGE, REFORM AND ACCOUNTABILITY

BLACK LIVES MATTER

As I write this, thousands of protestors all around the world are marching against institutionalized racism and police brutality. We see the power of social media in reaction to the video of the killing of George Floyd, a Black man killed in Minneapolis by police officer Derek Chauvin. With his shades on top of his head, undisturbed—meaning there was no resistance—Chauvin knelt casually with his hand in his pocket on George Floyd's neck for nearly nine minutes as he gasped for air pleading, "I can't breathe." While onlookers pleaded for his mercy, fellow officers simply watched as George Floyd had the life suffocated out of his body.

Being Black in America, we know all too well that there's no place to run, no place to hide, no place to truly be safe. We live in constant fear of law enforcement officials armed with weapons, who monitor our every move and attack us on the street or in our homes, killing us for the slightest alleged provocation.

The birth and development of the American police force can be traced to a multitude of historical, legal, political and economic conditions. The institution of slavery and the control of minorities were two of the more formidable historic features shaping early American policing.

Slave patrols and Night Watches, which later became modern police departments, were both designed to control the behaviors of minorities. The similarities between the slave patrols and modern American policing are too familiar to dismiss or ignore and should be considered a forerunner of modern American law enforcement. The legacy of slavery and racism did not end after the Civil War. In fact, it can be argued that extreme violence against people of color became even worse with the rise of vigilante groups who resisted Reconstruction. Perhaps the most infamous American vigilante group, the Ku Klux Klan, started in the 1860s, was notorious for assaulting and lynching Black men for transgressions that would not be considered crimes had a White man committed them. Lynching occurred across the entire country, not just in the South. In 1871, Congress passed the Ku Klux Klan Act, which prohibited states from violating the Civil Rights of all citizens. But due to law enforcements' involvement with the infamous group, this legislation did not stem the tide of racial or ethnic abuse that persisted well into the 1960s.

Today's law enforcement is more diverse, but the harassment, abuse and even death stemming from racial profiling remain the same. In today's society, you're likely to be recorded, since just about everyone is armed with a mobile device. But still, it appears that most officers really don't care, based on the frequency in which we see police misconduct. It's almost as if officers are rewarded with paid administrated leave during what, more often than not, appears to be a bogus investigation trying to assassinate the character of the victim as opposed to addressing the crime at hand.

There have been more than 5,000 fatal police shootings by an on-duty police officer in the United States since 2015. After Michael Brown, an unarmed Black man, was killed in 2014 by police in

Ferguson, Missouri, a *Washington Post* investigation found that the FBI undercounted fatal police shootings by more than half, because reporting this data is voluntary and many departments fail to do so.

But now maybe the world has finally had enough, with millions of people marching in the streets to denounce racial bias and police misconduct. People of all colors are shouting Black Lives Matter!

Say their names: George Floyd, Breonna Taylor, Ahmed Aubrey, Rayshard Brooks, Archie Elliott, Gary Hopkins Jr., Prince Jones, Eric Garner, John Crawford, Dante Parker, Trayvon Martin, Laquan McDonald, Ezell Ford, Walter Scott, Akai Gurley, Alton Sterling, Sandra Bland, Darrius Stewart, Tamir Rice, Natasha McKenna, Alonzo Smith, Philando Castile, Terence Crutcher, Freddy Gray, Walter Scott, William Chapman III—the list goes on and on and on...

I am determined to remain open and keep growing while honoring the revolutionary spirit that is me. These thoughts I share are my conversations with God, a connection that continues to awaken and lift me up. It's my hope that with my words, you've been influenced to reach higher levels of consciousness and become an idealist who refuses to remain stuck inside a societal box.

So is my word that goes out from my mouth: It will not return to me empty, but will accomplish what I desire and achieve the purpose for which I sent it. (Isaiah 55:10-11)

Poetry

Love is Revolutionary

As mentioned, I once co-hosted an event known as conversation poetry back when I first started to write, and every week we'd share poems so to stir up conversation. On this particular night, the topic was love. I told the event lead that I had no love poems, and everything I had written was Black uplift and Revolutionary. She replied, "Love is Revolutionary."

I stood there, mesmerized as my creative spirit was ignited. This was one of my first written and performed poems. It has been re-edited and altered many times since, but its meaning has remained the same, and it speaks to the revolution that continues to occur within me.

Love is Revolutionary; there's tremendous POWER in LOVE!

Contrary to the misinformed belief of some who associate the civil or rather human rights movement sparked by Malcolm as violent, due to him "making it plain" in speaking our frustrations during a time when America didn't practice what it preached... I'm reminded of a tree growing tall and strong as its roots grow deep,

We, too, become stronger, wiser and are able to rise much higher when we stay deeply rooted in love...

Humanity now stands @the crossroads between two different futures "Love & hate" God grace plants seeds of Greatness within us all and for me, poetry is my guide to life and God's light, revealed to me, his creative gift...

That I choose to use as a tool to break down bearers, here in a world, so full of hate...

It's time for Revolution and "No" it will not be televised... Rather this Revolution must be internal. For many when they hear the term Revolution, it's easily associated with violence, protest, Rebellion or even bloodshed. But actually, revolution is defined as making a drastic change, like maybe? A change in your thinking, which just might require *drastic measures... Was not Jesus a Revolutionary who drastically changed our fate, in the name of Love? Often times, people prefer their optical Illusion of what they choose to see... Spend far too much time existing in the minds of others... Without any real insight, besides a distorted stereotype, based on what they think they see on the surface. Whereas showing LOVE, RESPECT and APPRECIATION... Takes a conscious effort and those who refuse to adhere to LOVE, God's most POWERFUL blessing... Often times reside inside of a glass house, weary of stones being thrown "Due" to their choice to Worship the spirit of FEAR, over dramatizer of reality, often these persons are emotionally unstable as oppose to honoring the awareness of the beauty of our mere existence and take it from me... An Angry Black Man who uses the power of poetry as a means of therapy, serving as the master key in unlocking the gates to my happiness, although the cold winds continue to blow and send shivers running up my spine... l stay determined to "Keep on" push-in, mentally focused to peel back those layers of rough exterior, so to expose the Beauty of me... Because angry people cannot create a peaceful planet and I seek to do my part in generating peace! So please join me, by drastically changing your thinking, by removing all barriers that block your vision, so we all are able to be reflections of God... Was not Jesus a Revolutionary In the name of love...*

Darrick is available for book signings, speaking engagements, etc.
www.darrickajohnson.com
daricjohnson63@gmail.com

www.ingramcontent.com/pod-product-compliance
Lightning Source LLC
Chambersburg PA
CBHW071132090426
42736CB00012B/2102